Of
NOBLE
Character

Of
NOBLE
Character

Olive Coleson

Laura Emerson

Marie Evatt

Lois Fletcher

Ann Glenn

Evvy Hay

Kathryn Hillen

Mary Faith Jennings

JoAnne Lyon

Gipsie Miller

Nancy Swauger

Virginia Wright

Edited by Joy Bray

Table of Contents

Mrs. Charles Cowman
    by Laura S. Emerson 9
Flora Belle Slater
    by Virginia Wright 19
Ruth Pierson
    by Evvy Hay 31
Myrtle Hite
    by Lois Fletcher 41
Lois Swauger
    by Nancy P. Swauger 51
E. Blanche Cunningham
    by Gipsie Miller 63
Cecil M. Maynard
    by Ann Glenn 73
Ruth Kelley Argo
    by Marie Evatt 83
Ruth Sension Liddick
    by Olive Coleson 91
Myrtle Carter
    by JoAnne Lyon 103
Dovie Glover Gibson
    by Mary Faith Jennings 113
Ruby Reisdorph
    by Kathryn Hillen 123

A [woman] of noble character who can find?
She is worth far more than rubies. . . .
Many women do noble things,
but you surpass them all.

Proverbs 31:10,29 NIV

About the authors . . .

Olive Coleson, Marion, Indiana, is a free-lance writer and teaches Sunday school in a local nursing home. She and her husband, Ralph, served as Wesleyan missionaries to India and Sierra Leone.

Laura Emerson, Marion, Indiana, taught speech at Marion College, Marion, Indiana, before her retirement. She is a member of the Wesleyan Women International reading review committee.

Marie Evatt, Indianapolis, Indiana, served as a Wesleyan missionary in Sierra Leone for nearly 25 years. Since 1976, she has served as general director of Wesleyan Women International.

Lois Fletcher, Marion, Indiana, taught for many years in the public schools in her hometown area of Emily, Minnesota, before becoming general director of YMWB in 1977.

Ann Glenn, Indianapolis, Indiana, is Curriculum Editor for the Department of Local Church Education. Her YMWB book, *Mother T*, was selected as the first reading course book for the Wesleyan women of Sierra Leone.

Evvy Hay, former Wesleyan missionary to Sierra Leone, works with MAP (Medical Assistance Program) in Ecuador. She provides in-service training for Christian medical workers in Latin America.

Kathryn Hillen lives with her husband, John, in Janesville, Iowa. She has written *MEMORIES: A Present from the Past,* published by Zondervan (1987).

Mary Faith Jennings, Brevard, North Carolina, and her husband, Lowell, served as Wesleyan missionaries to India and Sierra Leone. She travels thousands of miles annually with her husband in his work for the church.

JoAnne Lyon, Facilitator of Lay Ministries of Warrenton Wesleyan Church, Warrenton, Missouri, serves on the board of Hephzibah Children's Home and is a part-time lecturer at Asbury Theological Seminary.

Gipsie Miller, lives with her husband, Dewey, in Charlotte, North Carolina. After over 40 years of active leadership in WWI/YMWB, she is officially retired but is active in teaching Bible studies and writing.

Nancy Swauger, Indianapolis, Indiana, travels with her husband, Paul, as part of the Wesleyan World Missions Metro-Move team, helping to train national leaders in church planting and evangelism.

Virginia Wright, Indianapolis, Indiana, is an active speaker and writer. She and her husband, Wayne, served as Wesleyan missionaries to the Philippines for many years.

Mrs. Charles Cowman

by Laura S. Emerson

One of the books which helped to quicken my faith and establish me in my spiritual journey was a daily devotional entitled *Streams in the Desert* by Mrs. Charles Cowman. Read, marked, and reread, I still turn to it for those treasured passages so practical and inspiring which deepened my understanding of God's purpose in my life.

How did the writer and compiler become such a close follower of her Lord? Where did she gain those rich insights of spiritual truths? I did not get to meet her until she was a widow, 71, speaking at the World Sunday School Convention in Mexico City where I was a delegate. This was in July, 1941, just five months before Pearl Harbor.

I can still picture her standing there, "pleasingly plump," in her tailored dress and becoming hat, with face alight, and a lilt in her voice, as she graphically described her recent experiences. Holding us captive, she told of the word the Lord had given her about Emperor Hailie Selassie, then an exile in England while his country of Ethiopia was closed. He had heard of her work in Egypt and other nations, and sent her an invitation to have lunch with him and his royal family during her visit in England.

Womanlike, she told us her first thought was, "What should I wear to appear before His Imperial Majesty?" Even her best dress would not be appropriate. She had no extra funds. Characteristically, she took the matter to her Heavenly Father in prayer. In the meantime, a former friend of her husband learned she was in London, looked her up and gave her 10 pounds for any special need.

The Spirit directed her to Psalm 45:13-14: "The King's daughter is all glorious within: her clothing is of wrought gold. She shall be brought unto the King in raiment of needlework." In a nearby dress shop she found a simple black dinner dress, just her size, with gold threads woven throughout, set off with a soft white yoke of needlework! To this she added a black velour hat and suede shoes. The total cost? Ten pounds! Now she could accept the Emperor's invitation with confidence.

Not until nearly midnight before the day of the royal audience, did God reveal why she was being sent to the Emperor. God gave her a definite message for him.

When she and her friends arrived at the estate where His Imperial Majesty and his family resided, two Ethiopian servants escorted them into a special room to be presented to him. At that time, Selassie, descendant of King Solomon and the Queen of Sheba, was without even an army. Mussolini had crossed over into Ethiopian Territory seeking to make the country an Italian province.

Fearlessly, she told us, she stood before the Emperor confident of the word of the Lord. With one of the princesses serving as interpreter, she revealed to him that he would be restored to his throne. Her prophecy was based on Isaiah 54:7,10: "For a small moment have I forsaken thee; but with great mercies will I gather thee . . . For the mountains shall depart." As God's messenger, she dared to tell him that he would be restored to his throne. At that time this prophecy seemed utterly impossible. It was later fulfilled, although Ethiopia is communistic today.

After greetings and a bountiful dinner where the family could discuss spiritual things, she presented the Emperor with a leatherbound copy of *Streams in the Desert,* and gave copies of *Daily Light* to each of the princesses. Before she left, he presented her with an exquisite ring made of heavy Abyssinian gold known as the gold of Ophir. Wearing this ring on her finger, she lifted her hand upward as she told us she often wore it at night while she prayed for the Emperor and his people. She had been the only person in England to tell him about the Lord Jesus.

This incident so dramatically shared, is only one of many revealing her mature life of faith, prayer, and devotion. She herself had written: "A beautiful life is one that fulfills its mission in this world, and does what God made it to do." This was her secret.

I wanted to learn what providences had caused a young socialite to be transformed into this Spirit-filled handmaiden of the Lord who entrusted her with His messages.

Lettie Burd was born into a well-to-do banker's home on an 800-acre estate in Iowa – my home state. The youngest of a family with grown brothers and sisters, every cultural advantage of pleasure and luxury seemed to be hers with the prospect of a musical career. At 19, she chose instead to marry her girlhood sweetheart, Charles Cowman, 21. Though he was not one of her drawing-room friends as the suitor she rejected, he was an outstanding Western Union Telegraph operator then managing the Colorado office. When transferred to Chicago, they had a beautiful home with a wide circle of charming friends. Although her life was most proper, she later wrote that she was "full of the world, the flesh, and the devil."

In His "prevenient grace" God was working out a better plan for their lives. A handbill was dropped at the Cowman's door with an invitation to hear a converted opera star sing in a nearby church. Since grand opera was one of her delights, she attended the service one evening. As this guest was singing "The Ninety and Nine," tears coursed down her cheeks. She realized for the first time that she was the lost sheep. Determined never to come back again, she somehow felt drawn to the church, and a few nights later, a Christian woman sitting close by led her to the altar. From modern paganism, God brought her into His marvelous light. These two women, now unknown, may never have realized what a jewel God had redeemed!

Her husband ridiculed the idea of anything religious. It was not until a month later that he surrendered to Christ. After five years of marriage they were now united in a fervent purpose to live wholly for Christ.

At a missionary convention in Moody Church with Dr. A. B. Simpson as speaker, they listened to the account of a young businessman who with his wife and child were going to Africa depending only upon God to supply their needs. Deeply moved, Charles put a roll of bills representing a month's salary into the offering plate. When a second offering was announced, he gave his solid gold watch and chain, and looked meaningfully at his wife's diamond ring. She surrendered it. At a call for missionary volunteers, they both stood. From that time on, they became an effective gospel team. Professionally, she surrendered her given name and chose to be called Mrs. Charles Cowman.

How definitely God was preparing them for a life of sacrificial missionary service. As wire Chief in his office, Charles had nearly 600 men working under him. Many of them he won to Christ. They lost their taste for opera and secular music and novels, and chose an out-and-out walk with God.

One morning as she rose early for devotions, she became conscious of an "Unseen Presence" near her. Hushed, she knew that the Holy Spirit had come to abide with her forever. Now divinely equipped, immersed in infinite love, she arose to seek only God's will and His way.

Soon this devoted couple exchanged his lucrative executive position and her social life for Bible school. They felt definitely led to serve abroad without any mission board backing, and went to Japan in 1908 by faith – obtaining promises, praying in funds, training new helpers, and establishing a Bible school – all at a strenuous pace. Charles felt directed by the Holy Spirit to launch an "Every Creature Literature Crusade," taking the gospel message to every home in Japan. This vision grew into the organization of the Oriental Missionary Society.

After ten encouraging years, they were forced to return to the United States as the pressures and responsibilities took their toll on his health. With no home in which to recuperate, they were deeded a "little brown bungalow" in Los Angeles by one of his former telegraph friends.

All of us know something of suffering, sorrow, and heartache in our lifetime. The question is, how do we react to it? How did Mrs. Cowman?

She refers to those next six pain-filled years as her battleground – praying, writing thousands of letters, struggling to get the message out while watching her beloved burn the candle at both ends. But every home in Japan received a first gospel message within 17 years. His heart attacks increased in number and intensity.

Desperately she began her search for choice quotes to strengthen his and her own courage. Faith tonics, she called them. She haunted bookstores for old devotional books with rich gleanings of others who had suffered and found comfort. She wanted God's secrets. Beautiful poems and sentences she quoted in her letters and diaries from the treasures she had read, underlined, and marked from these volumes. Her reading represented a cross section of the best in Christian literature from the old classics to the deep truths found in current periodicals.

They felt left to themselves as if God did not know nor

care. Then they found comfort in this admonition of George McDonald.

> To trust in spite of the look of being forsaken, to keep crying out in the vast, whence comes no returning voice, and where seems no hearing, to see the machinery of the world pauselessly grinding on as if self-moved, caring for no life, nor shifting one hair's breadth for all entreaty, and yet believe that God is awake and utterly loving; desire nothing but what comes from His hand; to wait patiently, ready to die fearing only lest faith should fail – such is the victory that overcometh the world, such is faith indeed.

All the powers of darkness seemed bent on destroying faith in God's love. The intensity of her soul's conflict is expressed in this paragraph she quoted from Charles Spurgeon.

> Our faith is the center of the target at which God doth shoot when He tries us; and if any other grace shall escape untried, certainly faith shall not. There is no way of piercing faith to its very marrow like the sticking of the arrow of desertion into it; this finds it out whether it be of the immortals or no . . . Blest the man who can endure the ordeal.

She refused to be rebellious, resisted the arch enemy of her soul, determined to be submissive. Both were fighting for life. God helped them to triumph and be strong. It was this period of heartbreak and waiting on God that enabled her to become such a sympathetic, compassionate woman of God.

For six years they waged this battle between life and death. A Christian nurse, Lydia Bemmels, offered her services. But in 1934, at the age of 56, Charles Cowman "fell asleep in Jesus."

> They had been rare lovers. Charles had written to her:
> I thank God for you, my loved one, as for no other gift of His bestowing. You cannot know what you are to me; no words will express it. Everything in our lives has gone like the unwinding of a golden thread.

She wrote in her diary, "I must look at the glory side. I must think of Charlie's joy." That was God's answer and hers. She found his last words to her written on a slip of paper in his Bible: "Go on with my unfinished task."

In deep loneliness, this widow, now 54, entered further into the school of suffering. Lydia Bemmels became her companion. When walking along the seashore one day, greatly tempted to wonder if even God had forgotten her, she noticed a little leaflet lying at her feet. She picked it up and read, "God smiles on His child in the eye of the storm." God had heard her cry, and brought peace and courage. "It was when my heart seemed breaking under the anguish of a terrible bereavement that Jesus was revealed to me as the 'God of all comfort . . . a living, bright reality.'" Feeling lonely and bereft, a sweet Voice whispered to her, "Pass on to other troubled hearts some of the messages that were helpful to you throughout the years of testing."

For three years she contributed a short devotional message to a religious periodical. Requested to publish these truths in book form, she compiled *Streams in the Desert,* sharing those ideas which had helped to sustain her. Translated into some two dozen languages and dialects with over a million copies in English alone, *Streams in the Desert* continues to bless.

Encouraged by others, she wrote her husband's biography, *The Missionary Warrior,* and began *Springs in the Valley.* Four years had passed since her husband's death, when Ernest Kilbourne, who had assumed Mr. Cowman's duties also died, leaving the mission in a crisis.

Through all her healing experiences and spiritual growth, God had been grooming her for His special assignment. A new chapter in her life began when she was chosen president of the Oriental Missionary Society (later named OMS International). This was in 1928 before the feminist movement and ERA! She was radiantly happy with her staff.

One secret of her ministry was her constant dependence on the guidance of the Holy Spirit. When pressed for the many decisions a president must make, she would say softly, "God will give us light on this. We shall know. Let us hold this before God in prayer. When He speaks, we will move forward."

After visiting the missions in China and Korea, she returned to America, her strength almost spent. When the doctor ordered her to take no more public services, fearing she might drop dead, she opened her Bible to Psalm 61:6, "Thou wilt prolong the king's life." Hope sprang eternal in her breast. As she prayed, the Lord told her that she could have His life until her work on earth was done.

She met her engagement to speak at the little Country Church of Hollywood in confidence, although Nurse Bemmels sat behind her on the platform with a hypodermic needle and other emergency needs ready! God had worked a miracle! She passed the test and would be speaking for many years to come.

Years after I had first heard her speak, I had the privilege of meeting Mrs. Cowman again. I had just lost my own minister father and took my mother with me for the interview. The two godly widows found much in common and talked of God's care. "Shortly before Mr. Cowman died," she said, "he told

14

me he knew that after he was gone, I would be very lonely. Read often 1 Thessalonians 4:13-18," he added. "God will comfort in His own appointed way, which is to watch for His appearing and the resurrection of those who sleep in Him. I would not advise you to spend too much time at my grave as it will only keep open the wound. The Lord will bring you triumphantly through."

She told me how youth had requested her to compile a book exclusively for them like *Streams in the Desert* – one with a challenge for full abandonment to God. She wanted quotations, and asked me to share some for *Mountain Trailways for Youth* which she later published. Since I had also been a collector of uplifting sayings which I would write on my blackboard each week in my classroom, I sent some to her.

Youth were especially dear to her and responded readily to her messages. Often she would wear the costume of the people she represented, her black eyes flashing, standing 5 feet, weighing 164 pounds. She kept fit and could still bend and touch her fingers to the floor at 63 years! Her spiritual sons and daughters numbered in the thousands.

With all her speaking, she continued to write, compiling *Consolation* for all the sorrowing. To encourage older pilgrims, at 82 she published *Traveling Toward Sunrise* – not sunset – dedicating it to Lydia Bemmels whose companionship had blessed her for 28 years. The proceeds of her books were given to World Gospel Crusades.

Relinquishing her executive responsibility, but still keeping in close contact, she and her nurse settled in a pleasant cottage only a block from the offices, rightly named "Oasis." Friends near and far called for tea or coffee and the spiritual inspiration of a conversation interlaced with Bible promises, her joy in the Lord, and a vision aflame for world missions.

Delighted with the preparation for the reception to be given in the new offices on her eightieth birthday, she wrote the booklet, *Life Begins at Eighty* as a surprise gift for her guests. Five years later, as her eyesight dimmed, she added *Handfuls on Purpose,* determined to "die working." During her final illness, she entrusted her files of quotations and books to her associate who edited *Streams in the Desert II.*

She herself was now facing the sunrise. Her Lord, whom she knew so intimately, called her to himself on Easter Sunday, April 17, 1960, in her 90th year.

She now belongs to that great cloud of witnesses who have finished their course and incite us to look to Jesus as we run the race for His glory.

I'm thankful for the inspiration I gleaned from this "divinely-fashioned" handmaiden of the Lord.

Flora Belle Slater
by Virginia Wright

The slender storyteller on the platform made me forget the irritating sawdust in my shoes. The sheer drama of her story held the crowd of several hundred spellbound in spite of the oppressive August afternoon heat. Her dark eyes shone with the intensity of her emotions as she swept a multi-colored Mexican serape from the altar and flung it about her shoulders. A huge sombrero was placed atop her smooth brown hair, and with a flourish, she caught up a shiny machete in her right hand and brandished it with authority.

It was missionary day at the southern Illinois district camp at Charleston, and Flora Belle Slater was the speaker. I was a starry-eyed girl of fourteen searching for a life goal. I found it that afternoon! God called me to be a missionary. Her pleading hands became the hands of multitudes of people reaching out to me. During the years of preparation when other voices called or difficulties seemed insurmountable, that memory of Flora Belle on that platform held me to the pursuit of my goal. She has had a profound influence on my life ever since.

I had no way of knowing then that twelve years later God would send us to the Philippines one month apart! Nor that in His incredible wisdom, He would allow my husband and me to serve our apprenticeship in missions in partnership with this master teacher.

God prepared Flora Belle for her special assignment by first allowing her to be a missionary child in Africa and the West Indies where her parents served. He gave her a call to missions during childhood after listening to her own dynamic missionary father preach. Then came school, teaching in the Mexican Bible school, pioneering a church in Puerto Rico, and serving as leader of the Bible school in Peru. Overseas service was interspersed with deputation ministries during which she crisscrossed the home church from coast to coast. Then finally, she suffered a serious illness and surgery which interrupted all activity and travel.

During the time of recuperation, she prayed earnestly for someone to respond to a desperate call for help from the Philippines. When God said, "I want you to go," she answered joyously, and was eventually appointed by the mission board to join Paul and Frances Thomas already at the Bible school in Luzon. She considered her appointment one of the most thrilling of her life. She was to be part of the ministry team to Mindanao where churches were already springing up as people migrated from the island of Luzon. Flora Belle was to lead the new Bible school which was already begun by eager Filipino workers. The Thomases were to move to Mindanao to teach in the school while he supervised the work of evangelism and church planting. As soon as strength returned, she began to prepare in characteristic full-throttle fashion.

When Wayne and I were appointed to the Philippines to replace the Thomases in Luzon, we moved to the mission home in Indianapolis to prepare for our departure. We found Flora Belle vigorously packing more than 40 trunks, crates and barrels. We learned that she never did anything by halves. One of her favorite sayings was her own paraphrase of a quote from the Word, "Whatever your hands find to do, do it with all your might!" And it was always delivered with emphasis on "whatever" and "all!"

During those hectic days of packing, we felt enveloped in her love and enthusiasm. Right from the start, we were family going out together to do the most exciting work anyone was ever called to do! One of the first lessons we learned was about what to take to the mission field. "Don't ever refuse anything that is offered to you. You have no idea when you might need it. And the giver becomes a partner with you in your work."

Literally everything from "soup to nuts" was going into her freight. We soon learned that her personal belongings occupied very few of those trunks and crates. Almost everything was "for the work." There were hundreds of books, musical instruments, medicines, linens, clothing, tools and hardware – all "for the work." It was a rule she lived by, and one she

20

expected those she worked with to live by. In fact, she simply assumed that if you loved the Lord and were committed to His work, you served at any personal cost without hesitation.

Who was it that did not take a furlough for seven years? Flora Belle, of course! Because it would not be "good for the work" to leave the new school just when it was time to graduate the first class. Her students were her "children" and she was, their "mother," and neither she nor they could conceive of graduation without her. And besides that, there was no one to take her place.

Who was it who always had just what someone needed to accomplish a task – electrical tape or shockproof screwdriver, or a certain color of thread? Flora Belle, of course! And she always knew just where to find them! She always had money, too, because she was a marvelous money manager. Even though she hated bookkeeping with a passion, she could give an account of what she had spent, how much she had left, and what it was for!

How she loved "the work," her students and her co-missionaries! We never saw "Auntie," as we affectionately called her, performing her task with the dogged determination of someone who felt trapped by a "call." She was commissioned by the Lord to prepare Filipino workers capable of establishing a mature, fully indigenous national church. She understood how strategic her success was to the attainment of the overall objectives of the work. We labored as a family united by one common goal. When new missionaries came to join us, they were received with open arms. Her love for each member of the family was demonstrated by her unfailing loyalty, even when she disagreed with us.

She had an uncanny way of sensing and meeting our needs, sometimes with laughter and sometimes by crying with us. When we faced heartbreaks in the work, times of betrayal by trusted workers, or spiritual failure among our promising students, she prayed and wept with us over the losses.

She also knew when we were taking ourselves too seriously, and needed to lighten up. She would reach out and grab her imaginary guitar and begin to strum it. Then she would sing in her best amateur country gospel music style, "He don't compel ya to go 'gainst your will; He just makes ya willin' ta go." It never failed to clear the atmosphere as we laughed heartily at her and ourselves.

Auntie entered into our family life as naturally and easily as if she belonged there. Wayne and I sometimes wondered

21

why she never married, because she had such a huge capacity to love and give of herself. And give, she did! Indelibly painted on the pages of my memory are enchanting pictures of Auntie seated on the rattan sofa in our mission home with our children. She spent hours telling them stories of her childhood in Africa in response to their pleas, "Auntie, please tell us another story." She even taught them to sing "There's not a friend like the lowly Jesus" in Zulu complete with authentic clicks."

If she ever pined over a lost lover of by-gone days, we never knew it. She accepted her singleness as God's best plan for her, and often jokingly responded to questions of, "Are you married?" with the reply, "Not yet!"

Life with Flora Belle always had its refreshing surprises. She hated sameness and stagnation with all the intensity of her sanguine nature. Things had to be moving, and she saw to it that they did! It never bothered her to throw away old ideas that didn't work for new ideas that might. God gave some unique techniques to this exceptional servant of His.

She believed that a diploma in the hands of an uncommitted, unsanctified student represented failure. Following her example, we all prayed for at least one Pentecost each semester in both schools. Spiritual foundations took precedence over every other consideration. It was here that Auntie's unusually keen sense of discernment stood her in good stead. She could smell hypocrisy a kilometer away, and her forthright methods of dealing with it sometimes left us gasping.

Just because someone stood up in chapel and said, "Saved and sanctified," did not necessarily mean that it was so. She looked for evidences! Dishonesty, pompous prayer tones, posturing for advantage, or rebellion were indications of something wrong. She knew the difference between tears of shame and true repentance. And yet she never gave the impression of always scrutinizing everybody. She loved, fully, obviously, and unreservedly, even while probing for the reasons for pretense. We learned that spiritual discernment was the product of long years of experience of dealing with people and living under the constant direction of the Holy Spirit.

It grieved her to the quick to discover a student in a lie. She carried him on her heart until God gave her a scripture and an opportunity to counsel. It was a technique she always used. "Never confront a student with spiritual failure until you first feel the pain of his lostness, even if he doesn't seem to feel it himself." Rule number two was, "Never confront a student until God has given you something from His Word for him." Watching her at work was like taking a practical course in counseling. We found those principles worked wonderfully well in our family as well as in the school.

One of her girls was up and down spiritually even after three years of school. She was a talented, brilliant student with much promise for the future, and Auntie bore her on her heart for months praying that God would reveal her problem. One day she caught her in a half-truth about why she was late in arriving from her weekend preaching assignment. It was the first crack in the girl's breezy front. Auntie waited and prayed.

During a chapel altar call one day, the embarrassed girl went to pray. She cried until there was a puddle of tears on the altar, and then announced that all was well. Flora Belle, who had been kneeling some distance away, moved over to her with her Bible open to Revelation 21:8. Laying it before her on the altar she said in her calmest deep contralto voice, "Wait, my dear. Read that verse – out loud."

As the smitten girl read, she hesitated and began to cry again. Flora Belle urged her on, "You don't have to cry anymore. God isn't looking for tears. He's looking for truthfulness." She waited for the girl to read it several times until it began to grip her mind and heart, especially the words, "and all liars, shall have their part in the lake which burneth with fire and brimstone: which is the second death."

Then Flora Belle asked, "What kind of liars are going to hell?"

In a small awestruck voice, the girl responded, "All."

"Does that include you, then?" questioned Flora Belle.

After a moment of deep thought, the girl began to repent of deceit and pretense. She was enveloped in God's forgiveness and in the loving embrace of "Mother." The spiritual foundation formed that day has lasted for almost 30 years of ministry. And it put the awesome realization in everyone in that room that it was impossible to fool God or Mother Slater! We learned that you had better not try to use her tactics unless you were willing to go through the kind of agonizing, selfless travail in prayer that she did.

A very keen and talented young man struggled to be sanctified. He had natural gifts for public speaking and could preach long before he recognized the serious responsibility of handling the Word of God. Mother Slater watched him as he returned from Sunday preaching assignments basking in the adulation of his fellow students. Soon, she realized that if this golden trumpet were ever to sound out the Word effectively, it would have to be cleansed of pride and self-seeking.

Aware of a spiritual lack, the young man went to the chapel altar several times, claiming to be sanctified. Finally, one day when he made his way to the altar again, Mother Slater sent all the students and faculty to class with this explanation, "We are going to let your classmate bring his problem to the Lord in the quietness of this chapel, alone."

To the young man now bristling with resentment at being left alone, she said with tears in her voice, "Son, you don't need us here with you. You know what you need to say to the Lord, and when you do, God will meet your need." There ensued a battle of monumental proportions as he struggled at the altar with wounded pride and anger. Flora Belle prayed earnestly as she watched out of sight.

After nearly a half hour, the young man slumped in submission across the altar. His shoulders heaved with deep quiet sobs as he poured out his soul to God. When Mother Slater saw that the surrender was complete she slipped into the chapel and knelt beside him with the Word. In a few moments the promise for cleansing was claimed and the Holy Spirit descended in sanctifying power.

After rejoicing with him, she said, "Now son, I don't want you to testify publicly about what God has done until I give you permission. And you will not be going out to preach for a while. When it is time for you to speak, God will let us know." Instead of destroying him, that experience was the making of the man who became one of the most outstanding leaders in the church. And he still calls her "Mother."

If people were her first love, the classroom ran a close second. Her own insatiable curiosity kept her reading incessantly. That meant stocking up at the bookstores in Manila or Davao City whenever she had opportunity. When sleep would not come, she read and studied into the wee hours of the morning. In the classroom, hard questions were stimuli for more research.

We learned from her that sometimes we teach our finest lessons outside the classroom. She seized every possible opportunity to share knowledge in the school dining room, her own living room, under the mango trees, beside the sea, anywhere. She demonstrated that one could be spiritual and love music, art, science, good literature, and drama as well as the Bible and prayer. Her "children" were always welcome in her home where they enjoyed her record player, magazines, radio, and games, or just good heart-to-heart talks. She loved for them to play hard as well as to study hard.

Auntie believed that some things had to be experienced to be learned. You couldn't learn to be a soul winner without doing it. You couldn't teach tithing unless you practiced it yourself. You couldn't establish a self-supporting church unless you knew how to trust God for the supply of needs instead of looking to the mission or America. You learned to pray by praying. Every student participated in weekend preaching point work where these principles were practiced constantly. And she taught them all by her own example!

She was a firm believer in rules, not for rules' sake, but for the sake of disciplined living, but she never handed out a set of school rules along with the registration form and the schedule of classes! We watched and listened as she deftly guided the students through several chapel sessions devoted to making rules about schedules, dorm and campus etiquette, social life, financial requirements, and even a dress code for class and public ministry. She had a wonderful way of helping them to see all angles of a situation before arriving at a final conclusion. Once a rule was approved by a majority vote, it stood until the group changed it. And everyone kept notes!

We learned from Flora Belle that it was as necessary to develop character as it was to fill the heart and head. She firmly believed that students who were unwilling to live by the rules were unfit for the ministry, so she constantly "encouraged" them to live carefully as unto the Lord.

She also believed that a student who was unwilling to do manual labor, no matter how menial, was unfit for the ministry. Therefore every student had a campus work assignment. She never paid a school cook or farmer or yard man. The students did all those things for themselves. She made it her business to be everywhere present during working hours to commend, to prod, or to encourage when the task was unusually unpleasant.

Once in a while someone felt it beneath his dignity to cut the grass, especially in the early years when it had to be done with a sickle or a bolo (long knife). One of her students had lived for a time in New York City. He knew how to type and thought his work assignment should be in the school office. Flora Belle felt he was not ready for such a lofty job, so she talked it over with the older student who was in charge of the men's work. They agreed he should do his stint at grass-cutting just like everyone else.

One day Auntie looked out her window to see him working beside the path from her house to the dorm. He was idly staring into space half of the time, and whacking away half-heartedly at the grass the rest of the time. Immediately she found a reason to go to the dorm. On the way, she paused beside the disgusted young man and said, "Remember, son. Nebuchadnezzar had to eat it!" He cut grass more diligently then, and after proving himself worthy was promoted to the office.

We learned from Auntie how to separate sentiment from tough love in the way she taught trust in the Lord. She put it this way, "Don't destroy the students by allowing your pity to overcome your good sense and the leadership of the Lord. You give them the most when you give them faith."

One of her early students was a young man from a Muslim home who was disowned when he became a Christian. When God called him to preach, He used a dedicated layman in the church to supply money for his school bill.

After he had been on campus for several months, Mother Slater noticed that his shirts looked dingy, although they were pressed neatly. She was concerned that he might not be as clean and careful about his personal grooming as he should be, so she called him over to her home for a chat. As kindly as she knew how she said, "Son, your shirts don't look very clean. Don't you know how to wash them?"

"Oh, Mother, I was hoping that no one would notice. Yes, I know how, but I have no soap and no money to buy any," the young man answered. "And as you have instructed us, I have not told anyone."

Auntie's eyes filled with tears as she responded, "I had no idea what the problem was. Wait here a minute, and I'll give you some soap." She started toward her pantry to get some laundry soap for the young man. Then the Holy Spirit checked her. "Have you not been telling these young people that God will supply their needs without their telling anyone but Him? Don't give him soap. Give him prayer support and let me supply the soap."

She turned back to the living room and said to the young man, "Son, the Lord has stopped me. He wants to supply that soap for you. He has seen your sincere desire to please Him and He will provide." She prayed with him and sent him back to the dorm to wait for God to perform a miracle.

In a few days the young man received a letter, his first

since the school year had begun. In it was enough money to buy not only soap, but other supplies which he needed so desperately. He learned a lesson which he never forgot. It stood him in good stead when he was a missionary to Indonesia and funds ran out. God miraculously supplied in answer to prayer and faith time and time again.

Today, her "children" are serving all over the Philippines in The Wesleyan Church. They are part of a growing, evangelistic, self-supporting, missionary church that is taking its place in the evangelical community in Southeast Asia.

Also the dream she shared many years ago of Filipino missionaries to other nations has come to pass. It seemed to be the most outrageous idea ever suggested when she said, "Some day one of you will be a missionary to another land," but it happened.

Then the day came when Auntie felt she should move on to other horizons, leaving her mature children and other younger missionaries to carry on. She went to give a helping hand to her missionary children in Indonesia. Today, the leader of the Wesleyan Church in Indonesia is a product of their combined efforts. He was won to the Lord by the Filipino missionary and trained for service by Mother Slater.

Auntie was a complex person, deadly serious at times but also possessing a keen sense of humor, wise but humble, calm but full of fire, loving but firm, frugal but generous, deeply spiritual but intensely practical. She could be dignified if the occasion demanded while inwardly chafing at stuffiness and conventionality. We have seen her defy propriety at times, jumping into the ocean for a swim when she felt like it, clothes and all. She loved to pit her strength against the power of the breakers, to be carried along on the wild freedom of the waves.

That was the Auntie we knew in years gone by. It was always fun to be with her, but challenging, too. She never let you be anything but your best self, calling out all the mettle you had in you. She knew when you were giving less than all. Her eyes saw through you and registered either delight or disappointment.

The last years of her life are being spent in a nursing home, that indomitable spirit imprisoned in a body and mind damaged by numerous illnesses and strokes. Now and then the old fire flashes in her dark eyes ringed by lines of pain, and the beautiful velvety voice speaks only a word or two. Oddly, she can still sing, "There's not a friend like the lowly

27

Jesus," in Zulu complete with the clicks.

Henry Adams once said, "A teacher affects eternity; he can never tell where his influence will stop." The ability to match wits and exchange quips is gone, but the influence of her devoted life will go on into eternity.

Ruth Pierson

by Evvy Hay

Which are the people who have influenced us most? Not the ones who thought they did, but those who had not the remotest notion that they were influencing us. In the Christian life the implicit is never conscious, if it is conscious it ceases to have this unaffected loveliness which is the characteristic of the touch of Jesus. We always know when Jesus is at work because He produces in the commonplace something that is inspiring.

—Oswald Chambers in *My Utmost For His Highest*

It was a cheery, bright "Hi, Evvy!" that rang out across the compound as Doris and I started down the hill to the hospital that first morning, and it was a greeting that I was to hear with the same unfailing warmth over the coming years at Kamakwie. Through the mango trees I could see a figure with short dark hair wearing a white blouse and skirt and tennis shoes. A nurse dressed for work in the tropics. "That's Ruth Pierson," said Doris as we continued our walk, "Our doctor's wife." It had been after 11:00 p.m. when we had reached the hospital the night before and we had gone straight to bed. I had come as a Wesleyan Gospel Corps volunteer to work at Kamakwie Hospital, not knowing then that it would lead to two additional missionary terms. Doris Scott, another WGC nurse, was introducing me to life at Kamakwie. Ruth, whom I had not yet met, had already made me feel welcome.

Chambers, Oswald. (1963) *My Utmost For His Highest*. Westwood, NJ: Oswald Chambers Publications Association, Ltd. p. 171.

Ruth was born the ninth of ten children in the Meyering family. Only five years old when her mother died, Ruth was first cared for by one aunt and then a second before her oldest sister, Mary, provided a permanent home for Ruth. Mary had already taken in two of the other children and her responsibilities increased even more when her husband died. The family had originally been Nazarene but when Mary moved to Holland, Michigan she rented a room just a block from the Wesleyan church on 17th Street and began attending there. "And that," said Mary, "started the whole thing," eventually leading to Ruth becoming a Wesleyan missionary.

Younger sister Esther recalls shared childhood marble games, "kick-the-can," summer camp, and blueberry picking in which Ruth ate more than she saved. Esther laughs remembering that when Ruth was sent out to burn the trash she came back "just about every time with her hair singed." Inherently mechanical, Ruth became the one to fix things around the house when there was no man to do so. Mary smiles over memories of the haphazard condition of Ruth's room as a child. On one "last straw" morning after Ruth had again left for school without making the bed or picking up her clothes, Mary shouted out the window to her at the bus stop and made her return to clean up. Extroverted and athletic, Ruth was always involving others in sports and adventures. Her favorite was baseball, and when a young man showed up for a date with the girl next door and found she was not ready, Ruth offered to play ball with him while he waited. Always active in the church youth group, her own social life was full because she was so outgoing and ready for a good time. But she was known to have "quite a few requirements" for a boyfriend, particularly an interest in missions. And if a male friend was interested in missions he ought to be a doctor. And if a doctor, then a surgeon.

Ruth had strong spiritual leanings even before her conversion at age fourteen. As a small child one night she knocked on Mary's bedroom door and simply said that she wanted to pray. When interviewed with her grade-school class following a spelling bee on a local radio station about what she enjoyed her response was, "I love to memorize scripture." Ruth had an early interest in foreign missions as well. In elementary school she drew a picture of a boat together with a map of Africa and the caption "I Want To Go To Africa." She saw slides of Wesleyan missionaries George Huff and Esther Smenge who were serving in Africa. Mary cautioned her not to talk about her plan to too many people lest it not materialize. Ruth followed her advice, although she never wavered in her determination to go to Africa.

Following graduation from high school in Michigan, Ruth went to Houghton College for one semester, largely through the influence of a best friend. But as Mary reports, Ruth "wanted to be a missionary and a nurse so badly" she left Houghton and, after saving money by working, went to Butterworth Hospital School of Nursing in Grand Rapids to become a registered nurse. Following graduation in 1965, she took some junior college courses in bookkeeping and typing which later proved helpful overseas. After attending Inter-Varsity Christian Fellowship's Urbana Missionary Convention, she made herself available to the Department of World Missions of the Wesleyan Church. Following the two required years of work as a nurse, Ruth went to Sierra Leone in 1967.

Fellow nurses Elaine Newton and Mary Jean Holcomb smile over memories of Ruth's energetic behavior and resourcefulness as a first-term missionary. She was unselfconscious about mimicking others to learn the language. Whereas Elaine and Mary Jean would "take a broom to sweep out the house," Ruth would organize a group of young boys for all sorts of tasks while she enthusiastically "chatted with them like a mother hen with chicks." If a load needed to be tied onto the car, Ruth would be up on top of the VW to do it. Her first term she did not know how to light a kerosene lantern, a surprise to Mary Jean who had grown up without electricity, but "she just tore right into it." Not inherently domestic, her contribution to missionary family potlucks was often four-bean salad or chocolate cake.

At the end of her first term she went home "to find someone to marry" and did exactly that. While taking photographs of the Wesleyan medical work in Haiti, Dr. Marilyn Birch, who served at Kamakwie Hospital in Sierra Leone, met Charles Pierson, a young physician who was also visiting the medical work. He became a Christian there under the ministry of Dr. Robert Lytle and expressed an interest in serving in missions. Dr. Birch thought he would be perfect for one of "her nurses" at Kamakwie and so corresponded with him, finally giving his address and picture to Ruth. Both from Michigan, the two finally met on Ruth's furlough. A dozen roses from Chuck shifted Ruth's interest from an admirer who had invited her for a skiing weekend to a prospective suitor, and Ruth's influence shifted Chuck's interest from Haiti and internal medicine

33

to Sierra Leone and a year of surgical residency. Following a year of separation during Chuck's residency while Ruth worked in Sierra Leone, they were married with vows including the words of the biblical Ruth. Six weeks later they left for Sierra Leone together.

When I arrived at Kamakwie in 1975, Ruth was already the busy mother of two young sons but nevertheless found time to help regularly in the outpatient dispensary. That autumn some 300 or more patients were coming each full clinic day, with one nurse present on each of two clinic lines to see them. Because of a measles outbreak the children who came were especially ill. For a newcomer, even pronouncing words for the names of such tropical diseases as schistosomiasis, onchocerciasis, and kwashiorkor was a challenge. The crowds, heat, distraction of hunting for medicines in the pharmacy, and variety of health problems were astonishing. But when the situation was at its worst, Ruth was at her best. At one point she would be out with the press of people in the waiting room calling their names to get them in line. Next she would be quickly working to check patients, pour medicines, and collect fees. If needed, she would give injections or package up medicines in the pharmacy. Through it all she would cheerfully chat in Limba with patients while making sure that the lines kept moving. She gave one the sense of an animated general during a strategic battle. When not scheduled to work, she often came down near the end of the day to help count and package the cash so the rest of us could finish attending to the patients and still close on time. On a Saturday, when the clinic closed at noon, she would often finish her own work and then check to help the nurse covering the hospital with her work. During a four-month period when there were only two full-time missionaries and one Sierra Leonean nurse to cover both the hospital and dispensary she simply said, "We'll have to work more. Bless our hearts." She then scheduled herself for additional hours.

The active role she had taken as a single missionary in promoting the growth of the national Wesleyan church through outreach trekking and clinics was modified somewhat with the presence of small David and Mark at home, but she never missed opportunities to serve when she could. When I first arrived she would wrap a longer Sierra Leonean "lappa" over her own shorter skirt, take along a projector and filmstrip, and then take me to the village of Kamalenka on a Sunday night for a church service. When a special need arose she had us all hiking down to Kathiri at 6:30 a.m. for prayer with our Sierra Leonean sisters. During a time of economic crisis she and Chuck helped Wesleyan pastors' families with funds for rice, sheets for their beds, and clothes for their children. When Chuck was not on call and could assist with the children, she was inevitably ready to walk the mile down to church for evening services or prayer meetings. For the annual Womens' Institute, Ruth would help arrange funds for food and transport when she could not attend herself.

One Sunday we took a van load of women for "Women's Sunday" in the Madina church, forty miles from Kamakwie. These were festive occasions which each church sponsored yearly. Women of the Kamakwie church going to attend were all dressed in bright gowns or the traditional lappa and docket. Thirteen miles outside of town there was a ferry crossing. We drove up onto the wooden barge and then the women got out, talking and laughing as the ferry-men slowly pulled us across the river using wooden mallets on the long cable. When the ferry reached the other side the women ran lightly and happily up the embankment like graceful butterflies with their gowns fluttering around them. Leaning on the steering wheel and without turning to look at me, Ruth said quietly, "These are some of life's best moments."

The most outstanding characteristic of Ruth, however, was neither her energetic contribution to the medical work nor her unflagging support of the national church. It was the way that Ruth valued people. All missionaries and short-term helpers were invariably invited over for a welcome and later a farewell dinner. During one furlough, when I took friends to their house in Michigan, Ruth had just recovered from the flu. Rather than cancel our visit we had a sheet for a tablecloth, vegetable soup made on the spot, and a memorable day of conversation. When we received a pay raise Ruth's comment was, "We have more to give." As I passed by her house at the end of the day going up to mine there would be a shout from the window to come in for tea. If I stopped by to report on a patient to Chuck who was on call I would be pressed into a seat and given supper. There was never a time when I was not made to feel welcome. In the evenings, after the children were in bed, Chuck and Ruth could often be found sitting in lawn chairs on the screened-in walkway between the kitchen and the house. He would have on his white hospital shirt and knee-length shorts and Ruth would have on the perennial cotton shift and tennis shoes. I would be clad in my usual pullover and wrap-around skirt, and we would talk about the events of the day. If the boys were still up there were chocolate milkshakes and a story to be read to the smallest, Steven, who never tired of them. Perhaps what meant the most to me was the eagerness with which Ruth included me on a family vacation trip to a beach house near the capital city of Freetown. We spent the days swimming, sunning, reading, and keeping track of the boys as they adventured. Fresh baracuda brought in from the ocean provided our suppers.

At Kamakwie there was no end to Ruth's practical helpfulness. When I was ready to travel she offered locks and banding for suitcases. If I was working on an inservice class, she had large sheets of white paper to share. When my sandals broke she sat patiently for an hour threading fishing line through the leather so I could wear them. When women came by selling cucumbers and tomatoes, she bought enough for those of us who were down at the hospital working. When mangos and pineapples were in season her large canner was available for my use. During our only joint canning venture, making dill pickles, we chattered away so much neither of us remembered the salt and we had to haul the quart jars out of the hot water bath, open them all to add the salt, and then seal them up again. Knowing that I was hopelessly inept at using a sewing machine, Ruth undertook to patiently stitch a width of sheet around the bottom of the mosquito netting for my bed.

Time spent with Ruth was never dull. During the dry season she organized fishing expeditions that resulted in the rest of us tromping over hills and through rice swamps with all manner of necessary equipment. My contribution was less often catching anything sizable and more often diving down to loosen a lure that had snagged on a rock. Following the trip there would be a baked-fish dinner at her house for all those who had participated. When the children were home from boarding school there would be a trip to the Maron waterfall or the Loko area gold mines where miners sluiced sludge in a true old-West fashion. Shopping for supplies in Freetown was an adventure, with cash for half-a-dozen people stuffed in your backpack, and Ruth sending you here and there for cartons of beans, cases of milk, bolts of cloth, and sundry other items.

Ruth thrived where others paled on the enterprise of "packing loads" to get to and from the mission field. She arrived with virtually everything needed for a three-year term and knew just when to supplement with cases of this or that picked up in Freetown. Friends coming to the field assisted by toting suitcases stuffed with cornflakes or lurching through airports with a large roof fan. Prior to returning to the field one year, I received a telegram from Chuck requesting that I bring a jelly used with the cautery equipment in the operating room. The telegram had an addendum that was obviously from Ruth. The Western Union operator chuckled as she read it over the phone. The telegram said, "BRING KY JELLY AND CHOCOLATE CHIPS." But Ruth asked nothing of others that she was unwilling to do herself. A suitcase I needed to forward to Sierra Leone was included with their family luggage. On one occasion I took ten boxes of hospital supplies to their house in Michigan to be packed for shipment and found others had done the same. Some eighty pieces had already accumulated.

Ruth thought and planned three years ahead and expected the rest of us to do the same. As soon as she arrived on furlough she began buying the large quantities of things needed to take back to Sierra Leone. When I visited them in Michigan to help for a few days following the C-section birth of Steven, a somewhat astonished neighbor brought over the ten loaves of bread Ruth had asked her to pick up. After years of shopping in large quantities it doubtless seemed trivial to bother with only two or three loaves. On the field she was described as a person who "sabi send" or one who knows how to send others to get things done. That was evident in a stream of notes, people, mangos, cucumbers and supplies that found their way from one place to another at her direction. It was a wonderful quality for the person who was the "station manager" in charge of repairs at the mission compound to have. The result was that our houses were painted, our cupboards hung straight, and the kerosene drums were full when they needed to be. In her perpetual hurry Ruth would often run through a string of names before she got to the right one. An instruction issued would come out, "Eila, Cheryl, Evvy . . . would you bring me that drum?"

It is, in the end, perhaps the small things that give the most insight into a person's character. The often-seen open Bible laying on a table. The letters that related all of the Kamakwie news which people away from the field were so anxious to know. The long-distance phone call in the USA that lasted thirty minutes because there was so much to say. The ebullient singing in church, in the dispensary, at home . . . all the more precious because it was slightly off-key. The

37

poster-paper sheets around the house with scripture verses printed on them so both the boys and Ruth could learn them in the New International Version. The undisguised pleasure at being in the company of the missionary family during retreats and council gatherings. The ability to simply not say anything about the disappointment when Chuck was called away from the family on Christmas day because a man with an incarcerated hernia came into the hospital followed by a woman patient toxic from a snake bite. The parade of young Sierra Leonean men that went to and from the house with messages . . . and stayed for meals . . . and grew up to walk in the way of the Lord and provide leadership for the national church.

Ruth was an example both through what she did and through what she was. She worked hard as a nurse to help people with their physical problems and as a Christian to promote the growth of the church. She reached out to people with genuine good will and there was nothing in her of calculated effect. As a new missionary she helped me in practical ways. As thirteen years have passed I most value that she simply sought out my company and made me her friend. Spiritually what most characterized her was wholeheartedness. Her determinations to come to Africa, to be a missionary nurse, and to marry a doctor have all been fulfilled in the Lord's time and way. Like Caleb of old she said, "I want that mountain" and the Lord has given it to her. And like Caleb she received it because she followed Him wholeheartedly. Without, perhaps, the remotest notion of being an influence, Ruth has been one because in the commonplace events of daily life at Kamakwie the touch of Jesus in her life has made her an inspiration.

Myrtle Hite

by Lois A. Fletcher

You, Myrtle Chenevert, were born in the township of Bethel, Minnesota to a French father and an English mother. When you were still a young child, your parents moved to northern Minnesota where they lived in a tent pitched near a stream. I have heard you tell that there were so many fish in the stream that you could go fishing early in the morning and be certain of catching your breakfast. How good those fish must have tasted after being cooked over an open fire! By winter, a cabin was built in the woods for the family to live in.

You were the oldest child in the family so you often had the responsibility of caring for the younger brothers and sisters. You walked to school each day. When it was time for you to go to high school, you stayed with an aunt in the city. The final year of high school was your only preparation for teaching. You taught in a small building which was called the "Crackerbox" because it was so small. Here you taught all eight grades for several years before moving to the Emily school where you had forty students, with all eight grades in one room. You boarded in the Dave Hite home. It was here that you met and married Glen Hite.

With no religious training during your childhood, you didn't experience God's love until you were a young teacher. When you and Glen set up your home together, you both determined to establish a Christian home. Glen was also a young Christian who had no Christian home training. Glen built a log cabin on the brow of the hill by Lake Emily. Here three daughters and two sons were born. You began early to instill godly principles into the lives of your children.

You loved to read, but there was no money to buy books. You did have your Bible and God became your teacher. I remember coming home from school to see you resting in a rocking chair with your open Bible before you. You actually sat at the feet of Jesus and learned from His Word.

You were unselfish, always thinking of others first. You had no money to buy dresses for us three girls, but you made over second-hand clothes for us. You always managed to have a new dress for me to wear to the Christmas programs. One Christmas stands out especially in my mind. You did not have a dress to make over, so you cut apart your only Sunday dress and made one for me. That dress had little pink flowers on a light green background. I remember how special I felt while wearing it. Although I didn't realize at that time the importance of your unselfish act, I can look back now and understand how you were instilling in me the principle of unselfish love.

Then there was the time you planned my first birthday party. I was only six years old, but it made me feel special to have my very own party. Five of my girlfriends came bringing small gifts wrapped in white tissue paper. After the party was over and my friends had gone home, I spread my gifts out on the table. We had a gasoline lantern on the table for light. There was no chimney to protect the lighted mantels of the lantern. I leaned over to look at my gifts, and my curly hair caught on fire from the mantels. The fire spread rapidly to the light tissue paper. At the sound of my scream you were there to put out the fire with your bare hands. What Christian courage and strength you showed! I know you thanked God that day as you held me close.

You were a quiet but cheerful lady. As a very small child I remember Dad hurrying home to say, "Myrtle, put a few necessary things in a suitcase and get the children ready to leave. We have the fire in the woods partly under control, but the wind is beginning to blow. There is a good chance that the fire will jump the road and then it will be out of our control and will head straight for our home. Be ready to go when I come for you, because we will have to run for our lives."

As I remember, you prayed while you gathered a few things together and began to pack. Those were uncertain minutes, but you did not panic. God was your strength. Very shortly, Dad returned. This time he said, "We won't have to leave our home. God answered prayer, and the fire is under control." Could this have been the time that you underlined Psalm 4:8 in your Bible? "I will both lay me down in peace and sleep; for thou Lord, only makest me dwell in safety" (Psalm 4:8).

For as long as I can remember, we had family devotions after breakfast every morning. We sat, not always willingly, while Dad read the Bible and then led in prayer.

When we were a little older we each had to take our turn to pray. In this way, we learned to pray. I was timid about praying in public in front of adults during prayer meeting. You suggested that I write down what I wanted to say and take it with me. Then when it was my turn to pray, I read my prayer. That's how I learned to overcome some of my fears.

You had godly principles. You taught us not only that family devotions were important, but also faithful church attendance was necessary. Even during the bitter cold winters in Minnesota, you bundled us all up and we went to church. When the old car wouldn't start, we walked the half mile to church morning and night. I remember especially some of those clear cold nights around Christmastime. The stars were so bright on those dark cold nights and God somehow seemed closer to me.

The wood fire crackled and burned in the homemade barrel stove, but I shivered in spite of the warm fire. You see, the pastor had come to visit. It seemed to me that you always discussed prophecy when he came to visit. The conversation led to the topic of Christ's second coming. Even as a small child of about eight, I realized I was not ready for Jesus to come.

After the pastor went home, the stove was filled with wood and banked for the night. I climbed into bed and snuggled down under the covers ready to go to sleep. But sleep did not come. Over and over thoughts raced through my mind. What if Jesus comes tonight? I am not ready to go.

One summer afternoon you knelt with my sister and me around the old organ stool. There you prayed with me and led me to Jesus at the age of nine. How well I remember the peace I felt in my heart at that moment!

You demonstrated confidence in God's ability to "work all things together for good to those who love the Lord." This principle was instilled in my life at an early age. One cold morning, as I remember, it was about 40 degrees below zero. The temperature in northern Minnesota dropped that low several times each winter. You thought it was too cold for us to walk to school and wanted us to stay home for the day. I was in the fifth grade. I loved to go to school and did not like the idea that I had to miss a day. Finally, you bundled me up with a knit stocking cap, heavy coat, mittens, scarf and boots. Only my eyes peeked out at the frosty air. My breath froze on the scarf giving me a white moustache. About halfway to school, I found a ten-pound bag of salt in the middle of the road. I thought that I had found a treasure. I was more certain than ever, in my child's mind, that I had been right in insisting that I go to school. This was the proof. You had taught me that, "All things work together for good to those who love the Lord." God knew the salt was there, and He knew we had need of it. I knew we didn't have money to even buy salt at that time. I had learned another principle from you – that God cares for His children.

There was no holiness church in Emily, Minnesota. You wanted your children to attend a church with godly principles. Several other families were interested in this type of church also. So you and Dad opened your home for services each Sunday morning.

The furniture was moved out of your living room each Sunday morning in preparation for the service. Plain homemade benches replaced the furniture. You made me feel proud to be a part of God's plan. You and Dad were certain that opening your home for services was God's will. You did not complain about the extra work or the wear and tear on your home. Your excitement and dedication carried over to me. I wanted to serve God with all my heart and to follow your Christian example.

It was during these services that as a young teenager, I taught my first Sunday school class. We used one of the bedrooms and the children sat on the edge of the bed. There were no extra chairs and no place to put them. When the weather was nice, I took my class outside under the trees for the lesson.

At times, as many as forty or fifty people crowded into your small home. A young pastor from a small, country, Wesleyan church came each Sunday to preach for us. This young preacher has said of you, "She could put up with young preachers and young people in all their zeal and total lack of understanding." But it was this young pastor's zeal that led him to preach God's Word to this group of people.

Plans were formed for building the Wesleyan church in

Emily. That summer God gave you an exceptionally good garden. You canned hundreds of quarts of vegetables and berries. You knew there was more than your family needed for the winter, but you also knew that God never makes a mistake. It was not until later that you knew the reason for the bountiful harvest.

The next summer the men began to build the church. It was mostly donated labor. You prepared the noon meal each day for the workers. Now you knew why you had canned the extra vegetables and fruits. At times you managed to buy a ring of bologna to add to the vegetables for the meal.

You had confidence and strength in spite of adversities.

Habakkuk 3:17-19 is underlined in your Bible. "Although the fig tree shall not blossom, neither shall fruit yield no meat; the flock shall be cut off from the fold, and there shall be no herd in the stalls:

"Yet I will rejoice in the Lord, I will joy in the God of my salvation.

"The Lord God is my strength, and he will make my feet like hind's feet, and he will make me to walk upon mine high places." Could you have found strength from this verse during the drought and depression years? The rains did not come and the garden was drying up. Dad loaded barrels and tubs or anything that would hold water onto the back of the old Model-T truck and hauled water from the lake to water the garden. The truck was loaded with the containers of water. On the way past the house to the garden, the back wheel of the truck dropped into the cesspool. The containers turned over and all the water splashed out. Dad had tried so hard, but there was no water for the garden. If there were no vegetables to can, what would the family of seven live on the following winter? Could this have been the passage that you stood upon and gained your strength from? Yours was a "but-if-not" religion which held even during times of adversity.

For years you were the adult Sunday school class teacher of the Emily Wesleyan church. You knew your Bible from hours of studying. You were well prepared and had a thoughtful understanding of your students. You thought not only of the Bible truths you were teaching, but how the truths might affect your students. You guarded the questions you asked and the words you said.

Many tourists spent their summer vacations in Emily. A number of them made the Emily Wesleyan church their church away from home. After attending your class, they came back each summer just to sit under your teaching.

On Sunday afternoons, Dad loaded benches on the back of the old Model-T Ford truck. We children sat on these benches to ride to a small community five miles from Emily. Here, in a small town hall, Dad led the singing, I played the old pump organ, and you taught a Bible class for the people of the community. A number of families attended and were saved under your ministry in this little town hall. Several of these people later became charter members of the Emily Wesleyan church.

"How strange, her face is shining!" Ivan said to himself. As he looked again, he was certain that there was actually a glow on your face. Ivan was attending a Bible study in a home. These meetings were called cottage prayer meetings. This was the first time Ivan had ever attended such a meeting. He listened closely as you taught from the book of Daniel. This was a bitter, cold, Minnesota night. You and Dad drove five and a half miles in your old Model-T Ford truck, with a window missing, to be with these people and teach them more of the Bible. As Ivan listened to you and watched your life, he decided that there must be something to this teaching. Several months later, Ivan became a born-again Christian. Your Bible teaching helped him become established in God's Word. Your comprehension of Scripture exceeded that of many. Your studies on Revelation and Daniel were outstanding. During an evening vacation Bible school, young and old came to sit under your teaching. Some drove as far as twenty-five miles one way each night.

You were an encourager and had the ability to make others feel they could excel, me included. You understood adults as well as children.

It has been said of you that your generosity and hospitality were beyond compare. Your ability to stretch food beyond the number you planned for, had to be a gift from God. Whether it was a neighbor visiting close to mealtime or a stranger needing a place to stay during a blizzard, your home offered a welcome.

You often provided room and board to pastors, evangelists and missionaries. They were special people to you. I learned to share with others in this way, and a desire was born in my heart to be like God's people.

No matter how many difficulties you had to confront, you had a beautiful outlook on life. You took your sorrows and disappointments to God and radiated a confidence in His wisdom and ability. God was your constant companion, not just someone to call on in times of emergency.

Your granddaughter said, "My appreciation for Grandma grew as I did. I remember, as a young adult, sitting next to her at a women's prayer meeting. She talked to God just as if He were sitting in the same room." Your granddaughter was only one of many who had faith in your prayers.

Your Christian influence reached into many areas. You served as midwife to many of the children born in Emily. Many depended on the strength and calmness you received from God. You and Dad were often called to the deathbed of a neighbor. I remember that you sometimes sat up all night at the bedside of a dying neighbor. When you came home you told of the difference between the dying of the Christian and the non-Christian as you watched them take their last breath. Your godly strength and quietness were a comfort to many. Again, I was impressed with the importance of being ready to die.

Young people and adults all felt at ease coming to you for help. You served on the school board, town board and church board. You were respected by many for your wisdom and ability to hold steady under pressure and they trusted your judgment. You often demonstrated God's ability to "work all things together for good." Your pastor of twelve years said of you, "Myrtle Hite was the wisest woman I had the privilege of working with on a pastorate. She had such good judgment."

You were a pillar of the church and stood firm among family, friends and neighbors. You were a godly woman who learned at the feet of Jesus.

You were a woman of prayer, and never ceased to pray for the salvation of your children and grandchildren. Two verses in Isaiah are underlined in your Bible. "Fear not, for I am with thee: I will bring thy seed from the east, and gather thee from the west;

"I will say to the north, Give up; and to the south, keep not back: bring my sons from far and my daughters from the ends of the earth." Your faith was strong and you claimed this promise throughout your life.

You set your mind to follow God, no matter what the cost, and because of that I have a rich heritage. Your unshakeable faith in God must have made you a woman after God's own heart.

Another promise you underlined in your Bible was Psalm

37:25. "I have been young, and now I am old; yet have I not seen the righteous forsaken, nor his seed begging bread." Did you look back over your life and remember the times when you experienced, in a very real sense, times of drought both physically and spiritually? Yet, God did not forsake you at anytime.

You were a sincere steward of God's grace and have left me with a real legacy.

1. You gave me a sincere faith.

"When I call to remembrance the unfeigned faith that is in thee, which dwelt first in thy grandmother Lois, and thy mother, Eunice, and I am persuaded that in thee also" (2 Timothy 1:5).

2. You gave me a sound knowledge.

"And from a child thou has known the holy Scriptures, which are able to make thee wise unto salvation through faith which is in Christ Jesus" (2 Timothy 3:15).

3. You gave me a solid character.

"Believe on the Lord Jesus Christ, and thou shalt be saved, and thy house" (Acts 16:31).

In his message at your funeral, your pastor likened you to the woman of Shunem. He chose the words "where was a great woman" from 2 Kings 4:8 for his message.

"Men today have their standards of greatness. They vary according to the personal tastes of the critic or judge. Sometimes it is according to the amount of wealth one has managed to accumulate. Sometimes it is according to the amount of knowledge one has, or the education he has. Sometimes it is according to the world's standard of physical beauty or prowess (bravery, unusual skill or ability).

"The Holy Spirit has a different standard for greatness. These qualities which are ascribed to this Old Testament woman are to a large degree applicable to Myrtle Hite. We are not here to eulogize or exalt Sister Hite. But we can, if we will, profit from the example of her life, and the life of the woman of Shunem.

The first characteristic which I would call your attention to is *faithfulness.* A faithful wife and mother, she conferred with her husband before she launched into something which could have cast a reflection upon both herself and her husband and the prophet Elisha.

"The second characteristic is *hospitality.* When the prophet of the Lord passed through the little village of Shunem, he was invited to have a meal(s) in that home.

"She not only had the gift of hospitality, but she had genuine *spiritual perception*. She was a woman in tune with God, and because she was, God could share special insights with her.

"Another beautiful characteristic was her spirit of *contentment*. When Elisha wanted to reward her for her kindness and hospitality, she told his servant, 'I dwell among mine own people. I am happy, what more could I ask?'

"The fifth characteristic is *stability*. She did not panic in the hour of sickness and sorrow. She knew where to turn. Immediately she set out to find the man of God.

"*Stability and faith go hand in hand*. She fell at his feet, her heart breaking inside, yet with confidence in God. She would not let go until God performed a miracle and her boy was raised from the death bed.

"I would like to paraphrase this verse and change a few words. 'And it came to pass that a preacher came to Emily, where was a great woman.' It was evidenced by her faithfulness as a wife and a mother and as a true Christian. It was expressed in her hospitality, as she entertained many preachers and evangelists who passed through the village. She was looked to because she had spiritual perception and good judgment. Things did not cause her to go to pieces. She committed her life to Him as a young woman. She followed His way for sixty years. She loved His Word, and she loved God with her whole heart.

"Yes, she suffered the pangs of heartbreak and grief, but she knew where to turn in time of trouble. And when the time drew near for her to answer her summons from the Creator and Redeemer, she was able to say, 'It is well. I feel no scare.'

"She was able to look death in the face and say, 'Open the gates. I'm going home.' "

Mother, my heart responds with thankfulness and praise to God for giving you to me. I concur with the pastor in his message of "Where Was a Great Woman." What an example you have left for me to follow!

Lois Arlene Cogan Swauger

by Nancy P. Swauger

The winter storm had been raging for days. When it finally moved eastward, the little town was an awesome wonderland of icy frosting and painted curls of powdery snow on the lucid air. Though still in the early afternoon, the thermometer had already plunged to 28 degrees below zero.

Inside her small home on Pratt Street, Orpha Cogan was making preparations for the birth of her first child. She had counted on the help of her mother-in-law, but when the time came, the grandmother-to-be had fallen, broken her wrist and was unable to come.

Landis, Orpha's husband, tried to hide his apprehension, but as the pains grew more frequent, he crossed the snowy street to seek advice from their neighbor, Rilla Moorehead. It was not long before Rilla, a sometimes mid-wife, announced the time had come to send for the doctor.

The young man started down the street, his heavy boots clearing the only path. By then the sky was clear in the low rays of the afternoon sun, but the bitter wind tugged mercilessly at each seam of his winter coat. The father-to-be bent his head against the icy blasts, hurriedly wading through nine blocks of drifting snow to the home of the town physician.

At precisely 5 o'clock, a cry was heard in the green frame house. Lois Arlene had made her debut, announcing to the world that February 17 in 1903 was much too cold a day to be born in Ravena, Ohio.

During the first few years of the baby's life, Landis worked at the nearby foundry, and later as a local printer, a trade he had learned in Cleveland several years before.

Orpha was a schoolteacher who gave much of her kind, firm spirit to each child. She was also a great lover of nature and often reproduced local scenes on her canvas, filling in the finest details with her brush.

The young parents took their daughter faithfully to the local Methodist Church, and provided a warm and loving home for her development. Even at four years of age, this gentle and inquisitive child was teaching her dollies her version of school.

Lois was barely seven in 1910 when Halley's Comet made a rare venture into the earth's atmosphere. One of her fondest memories is of standing in her nightclothes at the back window of their home with her younger brother, Howard, gazing at the racing ball of light with its long fiery tail. Their parents had awakened them in the night to observe a moment in history, and that moment was not lost on their young daughter.

A very special room in the house at 418 Pratt Street held special memories of childhood dreams and teenage struggles. There, in her bedroom, Lois asked God to forgive her sins and to become her personal Savior. The day was July 21, 1916. Then just one year later, on April 30, 1917, she asked Him to be Lord of her life. There her love relationship with God began.

In high school her dream was to go to the country of China as a missionary. So strong was this desire, that she chose the topic of China when it was her turn to speak in the regular Friday chapel. Again, as one of four senior honor students, she gave her high school graduation oration on the same theme.

In 1920, young ladies did not often attend college; but in this household, there was no question that Lois would be given that opportunity. Although finance was a factor, the biggest question centered around which college she would choose.

For several years the family had attended Sebring camp meeting where two ladies took a special interest in this lovely blue-eyed girl from Ravena. When they learned of her desire to go to college, they urged her to write for a catalog from Asbury College at Wilmore, Kentucky. Lois had never heard of such a place, but, with the approval of her parents, she decided to send for more information.

During her last three years of high school, Lois worked after school as a Linotype operator in the local printshop with her father. After graduation her boss decided to raise her salary to 60 cents an hour so that she could save enough money for tuition the next year – $300. She was so eager to attend college that she took two correspondence courses that year.

At last the time came to board the night train for the long trip to Kentucky. Little did the slight young girl from Ravena, Ohio, realize what adventures awaited her.

In November of her very first year, an epidemic of typhoid fever temporarily closed Asbury college, and Lois was one of its victims. Weeks of illness and high fever caused her to lose all of her beautiful black hair. Not to be outdone, she purchased a fashionable bonnet and around the edge she pinned the curls she had saved from her fallen hair. No one but her closest friends ever knew of her deep anxiety before her hair grew back again.

Even her friend, Robert Swauger, did not suspect that the object of his attentions was completely bald. On March 10, when they attended a school ball game for their first real date, her bonnet continued to hide her secret.

At the end of her sophomore year, Robert accompanied Lois to Ravena to ask her father for her hand in marriage. But the following January when Lois' health broke completley, making it necessary for her to return home early in the spring, she began to suspect that her dream of becoming a missionary to China might never be fulfilled.

Nevertheless Robert's love persisted, and on September 1, 1925, they were married in her home in Ohio. Their honeymoon was an overnight train ride back to college for Robert to complete his senior year.

The next day in their small apartment, they sat down to the lunch they had brought on the train. After the meal, Lois and Robert prayed for themselves and their new life together, and on that day established a pattern of family worship that would last as a daily ritual throughout the life of the family to come. Since both had studied Greek, the young couple found it exciting to use a Greek New Testament for their devotions. (Even now, sixty-three years later, Lois still uses this same Greek New Testament.)

Shortly before her marriage, Lois received a small inheritance through the death of her Aunt Myra, a sum which would make it possible for Robert to complete his senior year, but not provide many luxuries. In fact, Robert never learned until much later that his young bride's glass at lunch each day was mostly water with just enough milk to keep her husband from asking questions, while his glass of milk was always rich and creamy.

After Robert's graduation, the couple, along with their classmate George Warner, applied to the World Gospel Mission for an overseas assignment. But just as Lois had suspected, that dream was gone forever.

As the depression years came and their household grew from two to three, and then more, Lois' selflessness, along with a lot of creativity, helped to stretch the small salary her husband received as pastor to cover the needs of a growing family.

"Lois, you really must buy yourself a new coat for winter," her husband insisted.

"But why? This brown one will be fine for one more year. Besides it's such a pretty color."

"Well, at least get yourself a new hat."

"But I have a new hat. Aunt Nettie gave it to me just the other day."

What wasn't said was that Aunt Nettie had worn her hat for several years before giving it away, and although Lois had worn her brown coat for just six years, Mrs. H. had worn it the six years before.

In 1927, Robert held a revival meeting in Corey, Pennsylvania, where he met with a Wesleyan Methodist congregation for the very first time. He was so impressed with their interpretation of Scripture and the consistency of their lives that he moved his little family to western Pennsylvania and became pastor of a Wesleyan Methodist Church.

In 1935, he was elected conference president for the Allegany conference. This meant that Lois found herself alone much of the time with five small children. It also meant she was responsible for directing the family worship and setting the religious tone for the family.

Lois had determined that Sunday would always be a special day at the Swauger house. For breakfast she served cereal and the Sunday school lesson, and each child was expected to repeat the memory verse before leaving the table.

When Robert was away, which was every Sunday now, winter was fun time for the children to walk to church. Paul and Wesley would take turns pulling baby Martha on a special little sled their father had made; and with Lois's oversight, most of the time they were able to make it to the church without a serious mishap.

Each Sunday the family filed into the little white church and up the aisle to the second pew on the left. There they

54

sat, Lois with baby Martha; next came Paul with Virginia, the oldest, in the middle. Roberta was the fourth in line and big brother, Wesley, took the place of honor on the end.

Paul was a fun-loving child, and some Sundays it took a pinch or two from Lois to keep him sitting on the pew; nevertheless, they were all ready for a romp by the close of the service, and the trip home became another adventure in the snow.

After dinner came family worship. During the week each child had a day on which he was responsible for the scripture reading and a hymn. But on Sunday, everyone chose a hymn. They learned to sing parts, and with one of the girls at the piano, the family voices became a beautiful choir.

Sometimes family worship had its more humorous side. One Sunday afternoon, just as the children began to take their turns to pray, the family cat came to announce that it preferred the out-of-doors. When a soft meow and a friendly rub on the leg failed to get the desired results, the meows became louder. The children tried desperately not to laugh; such conduct was never tolerated during prayer time. At last Big Kitty had reached his limit of endurance and let out a prolonged "Yo-o-wl." By this time the children were choking on their giggles. When the last amen was finally heard, they burst from the house and rolled in the grass, laughing so hard they failed to see their mother standing at the window also enjoying the fun.

Most Sunday afternoons, Lois would read the Sunday school papers to her little brood and try to develop an interest in faraway places by making scrapbooks, which always included the pictures of Wesleyan missionaries. Bible puzzles and Scripture memorization also helped to fill the hours of the afternoon.

If weather permitted, a walk in the woods became a lesson in science, and on a summer afternoon, reading was done on a blanket under the apple trees. Through her eyes, the children learned to love all of God's creation and respect it as His gift to them.

During the years following the depression, Lois's responsibilities increased. Her husband had founded the "American Holiness Journal," and she again used her skill at the Linotype machine to help in its publication. The living room was turned into an office, the piano moved to the laundry room and a printshop set up at the back of the home. Grandma Swauger became the nanny and a young girl was brought into the home to do most of the cooking and housework. Lois divided her time between baking bread, light household duties, and the printshop.

One day she learned, quite by accident, that a neighbor enjoyed her homemade bread, so each week she baked a few extra loaves to sell for three cents a loaf. This became her source of income for missionary giving. Even with her many responsibilities, Lois often found time to be class leader at the local church, Sunday school teacher (which she sometimes did with a baby on her lap), and founder of a neighborhood Bible study group.

In retrospect, she states, "All good things came our way."

In the summer of 1944, Robert was elected General Secretary of Home Missions by the Wesleyan Methodist General Conference. "Papa," as Robert was called by his family, was in California when moving day came. The house had to be vacated, so Papa's brother, Ray, and a friend, Jack West, helped the boys put the household goods onto a truck.

When all furniture was on board, there was still a canary and a family of goats, a nanny and two young kids, Cinnamon and Ginger. They had become the children's pets and simply could not be left behind; so Ray decided to build a crate for the goats, not knowing where the crate would ride. The truck was already full to capacity.

When the crate was finally ready and the goats were being led from their accustomed pen, Cinnamon and Ginger found an opportunity to escape and headed straight for the main road, with the children in pursuit. A Greyhound bus which happened to be passing by came to a screeching halt, and the passengers watched with amusement as three little girls frantically tried to recapture their frisky pets and coax them back toward the house.

At last the goats were corralled and the crate with its cargo was pushed into the open trunk of the car. There the animals continued to provide entertainment for all travelers who happened to follow the little family caravan.

In the little town of Apollo, there was no Wesleyan Methodist Church, so Lois lent her support to friends who began a Sunday afternoon meeting in the nearby evangelical radio station. Before long it was moved to the school building and a Sunday school begun. Lois's responsibility was to visit the homes in the community, and that she did very faithfully.

Four years later, all general officials of the Church were asked to move to a central location. So in 1948, with a temperature of twenty degrees below zero and six feet of snow, the family moved to Syracuse, New York, the site of the International Headquarters.

By this time both Virginia and Wesley were married, and within a year Paul was attending Houghton College. With only two teenage girls at home and more time on her hands, Lois went to work in her husband's office as a part-time secretary. The rest of her time she spent calling on the neighbors and teaching Sunday school. Life was easier now.

But on September 21, 1955, Robert, the light of her life, suffered a heart attack while preaching in a revival meeting in California. Lois was far away and had never flown before so she decided to wait until Robert was out of the hospital before joining him. Much to her sorrow, a second attack took his life before she could make the trip.

Although Lois was a strong person in so many ways, she had always thought of herself as Robert's wife. She was his strongest behind-the-scenes supporter. Now he was gone and with it went her human source of security.

Just a few weeks before Robert's death, Lois had become friends with a young French girl. She had purchased a French Bible, and was reviewing her high school language study by reading the Scriptures. In her word search she had discovered that the word "lo" was translated "here I am."

During the long night after receiving the news of Robert's death, this translation became her only comfort. When morning finally came, she reflected on the assurance of God's presence during the hours of the night and wondered if it would remain when she descended the stairs to face the sad duty of informing the children of their father's death.

"But at the foot of the steps His Spirit clearly spoke to me again, 'Here I am,' " she later stated. And that assurance continued to strengthen her through many difficult days.

The family had scattered by that time. Virginia was a Wesleyan Methodist pastor's wife in Lambertville, New Jersey. Wesley and his small family were in Ecuador under Wycliffe Translators. Paul, his wife and son pastored in Cohocton, New York, and Roberta and Martha were students at Houghton College.

When all the children had arrived for the funeral (except Wesley who was unable to return from South America), Lois made sure a time was carved out of the afternoon for family worship, and once again the family favorites were sung – this time with even greater feeling.

Thou hidden Source of calm repose,

Thou all-sufficient Love divine,
My help and refuge from my foes,
Secure I am while thou art mine;
And lo! from sin and grief and shame,
I hide me, Jesus, in thy name.

In want, my plentiful supply;
In weakness, my almighty power;
In bonds, my perfect liberty;
My light, in Satan's darkest hour;
In grief, my joy unspeakable:
My life in death, my all in all.

–Charles Wesley

In February 1956, alone now except for her aged father, Lois accepted a position in the business office of the Wesleyan Methodist Headquarters. And in June, following her graduation from Houghton College, Roberta returned home to be with her mother and to work in the Youth Department at the Headquarters Center.

Just seven months later, in January 1957, the headquarters building was completely destroyed by fire and all general offices of the Church were moved from Syracuse, New York, to Marion, Indiana. Lois again found herself with a difficult decision. At last she decided to move to Indiana with her father, even though her daughter chose to remain in New York.

Over the next eleven years, and until her retirement in 1968, Lois continued to work at the International Headquarters in both the Pension Office and the office of the Women's Missionary Society. During that time her son, Paul, left for Colombia, South America, as a missionary, Roberta to Sierra Leone, West Africa, and Martha to Toccoa Falls Bible College. Wesley would return when leukemia struck his son, and Paul would return to become a member of the Headquarters staff in the Wesleyan World Missions Department in 1967.

But Lois carved out her own place of service. Although she was never able to fulfill her childhood dream of traveling abroad as her children had done, one of her chief delights was to be president of the local Women's Missionary Society and give studies on exotic places where missionaries lived.

That did not take up all of her time, however. Her neighbors knew her as a lady with a sympathetic ear and a warm heart for counseling. It was also her custom to sit in church with people she thought might be lonely.

Her blind friends were never neglected either. In an effort to expand their world, she secured "The Upper Room" and "Portals of Prayer" for them in braille. She also made tapes for her friends by reading chapters from the Bible. Sometimes the tapes began, "Let's sing together," after which she would sing a well-known hymn, encouraging her friends to sing along.

Each week she collected tapes of the Sunday morning service and her Sunday school class to mail to shut-ins. Her daily duties included phoning some of her friends regularly – one every day at 9 a.m. – to check on their welfare and to let them know they were not forgotten.

With her trusty typewriter she composed hundreds of letters to lifelong friends and missionaries. A special friend in a local nursing home received a note from Lois each week for five years. New missionaries often found a "welcome" letter awaiting them upon arrival in their adopted country. That was her way of letting them know her prayers had preceded them.

In 1972 a friend sent Lois an acrostic of her name and the words "happy birthday" using Bible verses. Since that time, so as not to duplicate her messages, she has kept a record of the acrostics she has sent to others for birthdays, Christmas and Easter, and she has averaged over 200 each year.

As Christmastime drew near, her sewing machine whirred over patches of fabric to construct lap pads and footies for the elderly population of nursing homes.

Children in Sierra Leone, West Africa, played with little black-skinned dolls, a product of Lois's ingenuity. African ladies learned to sew by completing the children's clothing begun by Lois. Arm bags to carry sewing supplies and Bibles found their way to the African women's institutes.

Kamakwie Hospital in West Africa received hundreds of rolled bandages and single sheets made in her apartment in Marion, Indiana, and cards of all descriptions were recycled to mission fields around the world.

For many years it has been her habit to retire at 9:30 each evening so that she could arise at 2:00 a.m., put on her "seven-league boots" (knee length socks she wore when praying), and spend two hours in prayer for her family and friends.

When Roberta was in Sierra Leone as a missionary, she stated, "I always knew that Mama would get up in the middle of the night to pray for me so that it would coincide with the beginning of my day."

Lois found it to be a wonderful time for uninterrupted prayer, and by the time she had finished praying, she was able to sleep again until time to get up for the day.

Lois went to live in an apartment at the home of her son, Paul, in 1972, and for several years alternated her residence between summertime in Indiana and winter in South Carolina. Her family carefully guarded her independence until 1983 when her health made it necessary for her to move permanently to South Carolina to live with her daughters.

She has a room of her own which has become a microcosm of her life. A large comfortable chair by the window is perfect for looking out upon the restful scene of a nearby lake. Mementos from many countries around the world, given to her by her children and grandchildren, are prominently displayed about the room. A bulletin board keeps her up-to-date on family pictures, both children and grandchildren.

She will point out certain marks on the walls which indicate the path of the sun at the winter and summer solstices. Even today, her love of God's world is kept keenly alive in her heart.

On a table nearby stands her typewriter, a new one now, given to her by her children. Above it hangs a large bulletin board with pictures of missionary friends. At 85 years of age, she still corresponds regularly with ten missionaries, especially the single ladies. Her letters of encouragement to all her friends currently number in the hundreds each year.

Beside her chair is probably the most fascinating spot in all the room. A magazine rack holds a Bible, a Greek New Testament (from Asbury College days), a French Bible (from the time of Robert's death), a copy of the Septuagint, a Greek/English lexicon, and several old hymnals, including a Lutheran hymn book with many of Martin Luther's hymns.

She explains, "My only purpose in using my Greek and French Bibles is to weigh each word as I read the Scriptures and not read the English thoughtlessly through familiarity."

Her family and many friends around the world still depend on her early morning trysts with God, realizing that her audiences with the Father have helped to shape many of their lives.

There is no way to judge the effectiveness of such a life. We leave it to the books of heaven to record.

photo not available

E. Blanche Cunningham
by Gipsie Miller

I cried until the wee hours of the morning. Then I heard a sweet Voice whisper these words: "And I will restore to you the years that the locust hath eaten, the cankerworm, and the caterpillar, and the palmerworm . . ." (Joel 2:25).

My flood of tears was the result of attending a home Bible class, taught as I had never before heard the Scriptures taught. I do not remember the home where the class met that night. I cannot recall what the lesson was about; but as the teacher spoke, the living Jesus came through the Word.

The atmosphere in the room was not emotionally charged by any means. So far as I know, others were not so moved upon. But for me, the room, the people and the teacher were all insignificant in the glory of His presence.

It was MY night! For the first time in my life, I knew that Jesus Christ could be met in the Scriptures. It was an experience far beyond mere emotion; it was a revelation to my spirit.

I went home to bed, but not to sleep. A girl in my teens, I lay there weeping over the past years that had been lost to Bible study. I was gripped with an intense longing to know the Bible and to be able to teach it as I had heard it taught that night.

Sometime before morning the sweet Voice of the One I had fallen in love with the night before whispered the hope of Joel 2:25. It was the turning point of my life! Things were never the same after that experience.

Blanche Cunningham was the Bible teacher of that long-ago night. Even though my mother, generally speaking, had the greatest spiritual influence on my life, Miss Cunningham was used of the Lord to direct me into areas where my future ministry would be.

I was living in Asheville, North Carolina, and was a member of the Wesleyan Methodist Church in that city. Miss Cunningham and an associate operated a Christian boarding house. In their hands, the boarding house offered far more than meals and a place to sleep. The high quality of that establishment attracted a clientele of deeply devoted and highly motivated-for-spiritual-ends Christian people. From this group came some good members and leaders, both for the local church and the district. Only eternity will reveal the impact these two Christian ladies made on the many people who passed through the doors of that boarding house.

My association with Miss Cunningham, however, was through the church. As superintendent of the local Young Missionary Workers' Band, she invited me to become her helper.

I knew nothing about YMWB or the work of Christian missions. The church in which I had grown up made mention of missions only as a budget item. So I really had no interest that way, but it was an opportunity to be near this lovely lady who had won my heart, and I accepted.

A wonderful thing happened. The stories she related of the trials and triumphs of the missionaries *lived,* not only in the minds of the children, but in my mind as well. My heart became aflame for the untold millions that had never heard the gospel. Soon I was one of the great number of ardent supporters of Wesleyan missions around the world.

Miss Cunningham was also YMWB superintendent of the North Carolina district. When she resigned that office, she placed my name in nomination. That was the beginning of my work for missions through the channel of the Women's Missionary Society, continuing from December 1931 through December 1981, with one five-year break.

More than sixty years have gone by since I met Blanche Cunningham. She has been with Jesus for a long time now. Yet the influence of her life on mine remains. She holds a place in my heart that no other, except my family, even comes near. She was truly one "of noble character."

What is character? Dr. Henry Ward Beecher said, "A man's character is the reality of himself. His reputation is the opinion others have formed of him. Character is in him."

Character is the sum of moral qualities that distinguish

us as individuals. No two persons are exactly alike, even in physical makeup. The Creator stamped individuality in the fingerprints of each human being, saying by this: "This one is unique. There will never be another exactly like him/her." The elements of character are in our constitution innately. They are the raw materials of our character nature. Character itself is also humanly developed.

Human character comes into its own when redeemed by the grace of God and indwelt by the Holy Spirit. Then the words of Jesus come true, that out of one's inner being shall "flow rivers of living water." In the physical world, the water of rivers takes its composition from the nature of the soil and the rocks over which it flows, and the surface vegetation along its banks. Jesus' analogy suggests that the Holy Spirit operates through human channels indigenously, in a way that is natural to the character makeup of each individual.

What kind of character did Blanche Cunningham possess? The first impression that most people formed, I believe, was of a highly refined, dignified woman, with a bearing of distinction. In mannerism, she was gracious. In disposition, she was kind and gentle. Possessing a beautiful spirit of tranquility, she had, along with it, a strong resoluteness in holding to her moral convictions. As she understood her duties to God and her church, she was utterly loyal.

I still marvel at her management of time. Despite the household routine of cleaning and cooking that had to go on day after day, seven days a week, for the large boarding house family, Miss Cunningham still found time for God's work. She found time to help others and to attend all regular and special services at the church. She found time to teach Bible classes and to preach as openings came, for she was an ordained minister.

I marvel at this because she was not a young woman when I knew her. There must have been days when her physical strength had to be carefully measured and conscientiously used. There must have been times when she asked and received a share of Asher's blessing: "As thy days, so shall thy strength be" (Deut. 33:25).

She never mentioned being weary or tired, at least to me. If she had, at that stage of my life, I would not have understood. The years for me had not yet taken their toll of physical energy.

But I understand it now. I, too, know the secret of waiting (Isaiah 40:31). God's strength does flow into the physically

65

spent and the spiritually depleted, and in that new vigor, God's child goes on, running and walking, not fainting.

This elderly lady had the ability to establish and maintain a meaningful relationship with young people. The chasm of the years was not too wide for her to cross to engage in the "give and take" of things that mattered to youth.

Blanche Cunningham came into my life at a time when I needed a role model. I had admired many good women, some active in church work. Several had shown a personal interest in me, for which I was then, and am now, deeply grateful. *However, there had not been one among them with that indescribable quality that called to something beyond the religious routine.*

My relationship with this lady, who made such a great impact on me, could be likened to that of a dutiful pupil with an esteemed mentor. She did not come down to my level. She tried to lift me to hers. I did not want her to come down to my level – to be "just one of the girls." I wanted someone to look up to in great respect. I found that in Blanche Cunningham.

For a time she was the human scaffolding around my spiritual life, and I thank God for the help she gave during those early years when I was first learning to follow Jesus. But in a building of brick and stone, or one of Christian character, the time comes when the scaffolding must be removed.

I remember when I was seeking the experience of heart holiness. Since I had not been reared in the Wesleyan Methodist Church, I knew very little about the doctrine. Consequently, I did not have it altogether biblically, and I needed a lot of help.

Miss Cunningham had been faithfully joining me at the altar to give counsel and to pray. One night she did not come and kneel by my side as usual. I looked up and saw her kneeling at the other end of the altar, a seeker herself.

Mentally, I changed gears, as this thought sent me in reverse. "I might as well go back to my pew," I mused, "for I cannot possibly get through to God without her here to pray for me!" To my mind, at that stage of my immaturity, she was the one with the direct line to heaven. Others around the altar, trying to help, didn't count. The line-up was "the Lord, Miss Cunningham, and me" – in that order.

At that point, my eyes were opened to the fallacy of this attitude. I saw that the road to the experience of heart holiness was so narrow that only two could walk it together, just Jesus and me. And together we *did* walk it. The Holy Spirit *did* come, and for more than sixty years, He has been my Guide.

Later, Miss Cunningham said to me, "I really have no idea why I had to go to the altar that night, but the Holy Spirit very definitely led me to do so."

I replied, "I know why you had to go. I would never have received my personal victory if you had not gone, for I was depending on you to pray me through." That incident was the beginning of a spiritual weaning process from overdependence on persons, however deep in grace they may be.

Time passed. A lot of changes came. I married. Life took on a different pattern as I resigned public work and settled down to the role of a pastor's wife. We moved away from Asheville to other pastorates in North Carolina and Virginia. Later, my husband became district superintendent, and then a general evangelist. Miss Cunningham went to heaven.

Now, from the perspective of years, I look back in evaluation of all that has brought me to this day in my life, and I have to recognize how much I owe to Blanche Cunningham. When her path crossed mine, my life was turned around – not by the woman herself, but by the Scriptures she placed in my hands.

I had been reared in church. I knew the Bible in story form, but I had never, until the night of that first home Bible class, encountered the miracle of Bible reading – the Living Word coming through the printed Word.

That is not all. She taught me how to live by the Scriptures. In long conversations between a spiritually mature woman and a spiritually hungry girl, the whole pattern of my spiritual life was set. Spiritual communication came through her words.

I'm sure Miss Cunningham never realized the extent to which the Lord was using her to shape my spiritual future. I was even unaware of it. But as she talked of the Scriptures, she witnessed to the strength of commitments, covenants, and spiritual disciplines which were the moorings of her life. I remember the radiance of her countenance as she talked of her *year verses*. As she shared this idea, it sparked a flame in my heart.

God's Word is likened to fire (Jeremiah 23:29). A spark is a glowing bit of matter thrown off by a fire, a tiny flash that ignites. In my case, ignition did not come at once, although the sparks were there in my heart. It took a long time for the flame of that idea to blaze into an active part of my Christian experience. Eventually, however, the *year verse* idea caught fire in my life.

What is *year verse* guidance? As Blanche Cunningham explained it to me, the *year verse* is a Holy Spirit-given Bible verse for each new calendar year. It points personal direction in some definite way and is obtained in answer to prayer.

When I seek a new *year verse*, I always begin in December to pray for and to expect it. There are four ways by which I recognize the gift of the *year verse*.

It is an inward communication made by the Holy Spirit to my spirit. Andrew Murray describes this communication: "Divine leading . . . by the Spirit of God takes place not in our soul or mind, in the first place, but in our spirit, in the inner recesses of a life deeper than mind or will. . . . In that inner shrine of our wondrous nature, the spirit . . . *there dwells the Holy Spirit*" *(The Spirit of Christ, Note C.* pages 229, 231).

It comes by intuition. Webster defines intuition as "1. the direct knowing or learning of something without the conscious use of reasoning, immediate apprehension or understanding. 2. Something known or learned this way. 3. The ability to perceive or know things without conscious reasoning." Webster also has an entry, *sixth sense,* "a power of perception in addition to the commonly accepted five senses; intuitive power." The *year verse* is intuitively received and understood.

It is verified by confirming Scriptures, which are succeeding Bible verses relative to the same truth. The *year verse* can be thought of as the trunk truth and the confirming Scriptures as its outgrowing limbs, branches, twigs and leaves.

Its end result is a compelling conviction that this is God's will for me for the coming year and beyond, for the *year verses* are not withdrawn at the end of twelve months. they are both cumulative and progressive and become increasingly fruitful with practice.

The rationale for *year verse* guidance is that the Bible is the Christian's guidebook (Psalm 119:105):

That while "all Scripture is . . . for instruction in righteousness" (2 Timothy 3:16), it also gives direction at all of life's crossroads;

That there is a particular will of God in both character and career for each Christian (Romans 12:2); and

That the Holy Spirit teaches and guides the Christian through the Scriptures (John 6:63; 14:26).

I don't remember when I began to follow the Lord in this way. However, I have diaries, journals and prayer books which date back almost forty years. I have researched some of those entries in order to show how the *year verse* plan has worked for me.

Sometimes the *year verse* indicated something new to come. In 1959, "As I was with Moses, so I will be with thee" (Joshua 1:5), was my *year verse*. I questioned its meaning at first. Was it for general encouragement or was there something more specific in this promise?

Intuitively, I felt it was something specific. Dr. Daniel Steele, *Milestone Papers,* declares, ". . . intuitions of our reason . . . lie at the bottom of all our other knowledge. They are the original capital with which our Creator has endowed our reasoning faculties and set them up in business" (p. 177).

Confirming Scriptures during the next six months deepened my conviction that the Lord did indeed have something specific ahead for me. At the close of the Women's Missionary Society General Convention of that year (1959), I was asked to write a program and promotion quarterly which the general executive committee was planning to publish. Intuitively, instantly, I knew this was God's "new thing" for me, and I accepted. *The Guide* was launched, and I wrote the contents from January 1960 through December 1966.

Sometimes the *year verse* focused on some work for the Lord which I was already doing. A memorable case was my verse for 1964, which was a part of Ezekiel 1:20: ". . . for the spirit of the living creature was in the wheels." Whatever the literal interpretation of those words, the meaning that came through to me was that there *is* a spiritual energy for Zion's "machinery" – the church's human organization and performance.

The confirming Scriptures led to Acts 2 – the coming of the Holy Spirit as the wind of divine energy. That year I came to know, as I had never known before, that this energy is still available, that "if we have it, nothing else matters; if we do not have it, nothing else counts."

It was a blessed year. My diary summary for 1964 states: "We saw something of the supernatural in the 'machinery' of the work this year."

Sometimes the *year verse* indicated a new personal enablement of some kind. For two weeks before the arrival of 1970, a great light had been playing on Job 32:8: "But there is a spirit in man: and the inspiration of the Almighty giveth them understanding."

The word that stood out was "inspiration," in its meaning as a "stimulus to creative thought." I saw the fulfillment of this verse in the help of the Holy Spirit in writing meditations for the Wesleyan Church Sunday school devotional quarterly, *Light from the Word.* The first copy was due in August 1970.

During the intervening months, my faith for the spirit of creativity for these assignments was fed by such confirming Scriptures as John 6:63: "It is the Spirit that quickeneth."

The day came when, as I was quoting the *year verse* in prayer and claiming its promises for the meditations, the Holy Spirit "sealed" it to my heart in a rare experience for me, of "laughing in faith before the Lord." This was exhilarating and yet humbling. Who was I, so utterly inadequate, to be permitted to offer a Spirit-touched ministry in writing these meditations?

This yearly method of guidance has meant many things to me.

It has deepened my belief that God has a particular life-plan for each person (Ephesians 2:10), which "will be the true significance and glory of his life" to accomplish, although no one is forced to take it.

It has given me a sense for the unseen. I have been gripped with the strong impression that life for the Christian is to be lived in two worlds, since He is now seated "in Christ in heavenly places."

It has given me a sense of direction for this world. Each *year verse* has been a deposit of revelation for my life for that year. Since I have had both chart and compass, I have not been lost in the world.

It has given me a framework in which faith's hindsight can operate, not in the sense of living in the past, but rather, in seeing the "Bethels" and the "Ebenezers" as "wells of salvation" from which to draw courage and confidence for the present and the future.

It has been a "workbook of life" for me. A workbook for students has exercises based on the textbook or the course of study. Life is the workbook in which the eternal principles of God's Word are worked out. Someone has stated the "rule" this way:

> For life's impossible situations,
> God has incredible promises.
> Faith makes the equation.

For me, "exercises" by this rule consisted of trying to meet the impossible situations in the lives of family, friends, or members in the churches we served and the churches of the district when my husband was superintendent, with the incredible [the seemingly too-wonderful-to-be-grasped] promises of God. My faith, too many times, did not make the equation.

Finally there came a day when the need was great, faith was weak, and feeling was in charge. My journal reads: "I went to bed and physical weariness helped me to drop off to sleep for a little while. Then I awoke and lay there, tossing and turning, voicing nervous, agitated prayers."

Then something happened which I cannot explain. Old words which I had heard others say, even which I, myself, had vocalized many times before, suddenly became eternally significant: "God's Word is true or it is not true!"

I jumped out of bed and fell on my knees, realizing that my faith had been brought to a divine ultimate – the Word of God, the scripture which cannot be broken (John 10:35). As I knelt there, I came to know how faith's equation is made: by faith in the inherent power of God's Word, not by "faith in my faith" for which I had been unconsciously striving.

That experience, like the one that happened at the first Bible class, was life changing for me. Prayer was on a higher level afterward.

In my diaries, journals, prayer books of almost forty years are documented hundreds of prayer transactions to the glory of God. Some answers came quickly. Others took years. Many are not yet finished. They have brought me to where I am today – one of the multitudes of sojourners "in the land of promise."

And so I bow my head and my heart in grateful thanksgiving to God, who send Blanche Cunningham into my life. She placed the Scriptures in my hands and then taught me how to live by them. I wonder where I would have been spiritually had I not been following the methodical, yet inspirational plan for *year verse* guidance.

I pray, "O, God, do it again." Send other Blanche Cunninghams to other Gipsie Millers.

Cecil M. Maynard

by Ann E. Glenn

Saints? What do you think of when you hear the word? What do they look like? Gray hair? Praying a lot? Sitting in a rocking chair? Arthritic hands folded piously in a prayerful attitude? Always mystical in appearance with "another world" look? Pleasant but never laughing out loud? Always in church or getting ready to go there or coming back from? Well, if this is your idea of a saint, Aunt Cecil was not one. Yet her life made a difference in the people who knew her.

In all her eighty-six years, she was not listed in "Who's Who in American Women" nor as one of the "Ten Best Dressed." She never married nor became a mother. She never owned a car, but said she had so many she couldn't remember where the door handles were on all of them. She never really had a home of her own, yet homes were always open to her. She was what the world would call "poor." Friends and relatives paid for her funeral, casket, vault and grave marker. Her niece, Mabel, served as her banker and never had to worry about any excess funds. But she made a difference where she was.

She made a difference when a young lad began as her substitute mail carrier. She was not only eager to receive her mail like everyone else, she was pleasant, kind, thoughtful and had an infectious smile which spread sunshine even on the darkest of days. He knew, this young man, that she was a devout Christian and if he ever needed help, she would be a good resource. Even now, these many years later as postmaster in their shared hometown of Alexandria, Indiana, Henry remembers her address – 816 North West Street.

She made a difference with pastors and their wives. It was not uncommon to be invited to her house for an after-church snack on a Sunday evening. There would be hot tea, crackers, cheese and pickles. Always pickles! She teased one pastor saying, "No one else can make as many cups of tea from one tea bag as you can." But her ministry reached beyond tea to tutoring, beyond cheese to challenging, beyond crackers to wise counsel, and beyond pickles to praying. When pastors left for home, they were not only filled physically but spiritually as well. Said her pastor at the time of her death, "She prayed for me when I was a 'little boy Christian.' When I was a teenager, her door was always open. She encouraged me to go to Bible school. Throughout my ministry, I often sought her for advice and counsel. She loved her God, her church, and her people – in that order.

But let's back up. Who is Aunt Cecil anyway? She was born December 10, 1894, to John and Rosa Maynard, the sixth of seven children. She grew up in the country near Alexandria, Indiana. She attended the Vermillion grade school across from the Vermillion Friends (Quaker) Church. When she was twelve years old, that church had a revival. Their teacher took the students to church for daytime services. Aunt Cecil was converted. Hers was a lifelong commitment to her God and the Quaker Church.

Following her conversion, she wanted to testify at church. So, she'd stand and say, "I'm so glad . . ." Then she would break down and cry. The next time she would try again, only to break down and cry after saying, "I'm so glad . . ." No one could learn what she was glad about. She never did get any further with her public testimony in church until after she was sanctified. Then she was freed. The next time she testified, she freely told everyone what she was glad about.

Aunt Cecil sang beautifully. Not only was she a song evangelist, she sang often in our home church. The songs, "It's Real" and "It Is Well With My Soul" always bring back memories of her. For specials she would sing, "Follow, I Will Follow Thee My Lord." She not only sang well, but could get good music from an old pump organ. Imagine her delight when she succeeded in teaching her nephew, Ron, to play it as well.

One time when Aunt Cecil was preparing to sing for a revival, she could not seem to find the mind of the Lord regarding which songs to prepare. Sure enough, when she got there, she did the preaching instead!

74

Each one paying tribute to Aunt Cecil mentioned her wise counsel and sense of humor. (Do saints really laugh?) I can hear her laughter when recalling this story. Her sister, Stell (short for Estella), got up in church to testify one Sunday morning. While testifying, Stell's dentures slipped out. Evading her frantic grab, they proceeded to scoot across the front of the church finally to be retrieved on the other side after being chased there by Stell. Grab. Scoot. Grab. Scoot. No one laughed. I was there. I didn't laugh. As children, we were not permitted to laugh at someone's calamity. A pregnant silence followed. Not the traditional waiting-on-the-Holy-Spirit-in-a-Quaker-meeting silence. It was the I-don't-dare-breathe-or-I'll-laugh silence. Stell said, "I'm not going to let the devil defeat me . . ." and proceeded to testify. How much laughter can one small, wiggly girl hold in? Aunt Cecil sensed how we all were feeling. Standing, she said, "Now folks, it's alright to laugh with Stell about this. We're not laughing *at* her." The congregation exploded. Everyone laughed – even Stell! It was not an unkind laughter; it never could be if Aunt Cecil participated. But what a relief!

Aunt Cecil laughed when she put Baker's Pain Relief in her cake instead of the intended vanilla. She laughed when nephew Ron quipped as the last syllable of the "amen" for the Thanksgiving dinner blessing was given, "Who opened the pa-monia hole?" (He was referring to the opened transom above the dining room door.) She laughed when she outwitted the over-zealous magazine salesman.

Children, playing church, pretended to be Aunt Cecil. Sometimes it was a shawl across their shoulders. Sometimes it was kneeling in prayer. Sometimes it was waving a white handkerchief. Sometimes it was singing a solo. But always, there was the smile and the laughter.

Sometimes she created laughter, like the time of the big snow. We (the Etsler family) had brought her to church as usual. We parked in our regular spot and proceeded to unload. That is, until Aunt Cecil stepped out into a drift, lost her balance, and plunged into it up to her waist. Now remember, we were not allowed to laugh at anyone. So, laughter was stifled. Smiles were swallowed. And we proceeded into the Quaker meeting house quite properly and sedately from all outward appearances. (You should have seen our insides shake.) Church began. After a feeble attempt to sing the first song, Aunt Cecil got up, cleared her throat, (Now remember, she was wet from the waist down.) and said, "Folks, we might as well laugh. You have to admit I looked funny then and I look funny now." Then she laughed. The grown-ups laughed. The children laughed. And there in that quiet, little Quaker Church, Aunt Cecil's sense of humor made a difference.

Aunt Cecil even made a difference in what she liked to do for fun. She enjoyed listening to Chicago ball games over the radio because she liked to hear the announcer. She liked to make artificial flowers, work crossword puzzles, eat Kraft caramels, and send certain Christmas cards . . . when her special friend was there to help her address them.

Aunt Cecil was always clean, neatly and modestly dressed – long sleeves and dress almost to her ankles. I never saw her without her black hose. I wondered why she wore them. No one else did. Then I learned. Aunt Cecil was poor. People would give her their cast-off mismatched hose. You can imagine how many shades of tan and beige she would have. Being frugal, she bought black dye. Violá! Pairs of matched black hose to wear. There were always the inevitable hair nets over hair rolled like a long rope and wound around her head. I never remember her with a hair out of place. Even her Bible had a black garter around it to keep it neat in appearance.

Her sensitivity and wise counsel made a difference. As I've said, our family had the privilege of taking her to church for years. One time when we stopped for her and were waiting for her to lock her apartment door, a man walked by on the sidewalk. He thought we had stopped for him and started to get in, cigarette and all. You can imagine the gasp coming from the back seat where we children sat. He quickly went on. We children had thought it was Aunt Cecil with a cigarette. Our hearts plunged. They did not stop until they had plummeted to the bottom, bounced at the jolt, and caused some nausea in their wake. When Aunt Cecil *did* come, a hushed silence ensued. Then, all kinds of commotion broke loose. We laughed, but with tears close behind. The distance between the two emotions was too much. She lovingly, wisely, and with a gentle sensitivity erased all our fears and restored our hearts to their proper location.

Aunt Cecil made a difference in children's lives. They were important to her. She stood near the piano counting out the time for more than one beginning pianist learning to play for congregational singing. Whether it was demonstrating an object lesson for vacation Bible school, teaching children's songs, or telling Bible stories, her love for children showed through.

When Karen requested we sing "The Star Spangled Banner," Aunt Cecil never embarrassed her. Instead, she smoothed it over, Karen did not know for quite some time that the national anthem was not considered the type of song to be sung in that little Quaker church.

Even though she had only an eighth-grade education, she was a voracious reader and made self-education a lifelong occupation. She was successful to the degree that when she lay dying in the hospital, she discussed the Bible with her surgeon thus ministering to him with her last bit of strength.

She was proud of her "children's" college educations, encouraging us as discouragement threatened to take over. She recognized gifts and talents in young children and encouraged them to make that the focal point of their life's preparation . . . schoolteacher, musician, homemaker, or preacher. She was never judgmental or pushy, just accepting and forgiving. She not only made the Christian life attractive, she made it easier for others to believe in God.

But the greatest way Aunt Cecil made a difference was through her prayers. I remember one year when it was time to go back to college and I needed prayer. You know, the kind where they lay hands on you and pray until the heavens open and God's glory rolls over your soul. Well, we were between pastors. I had nowhere to go for this. I had prayed Aunt Cecil would be in church that morning (She had been sick.), but she wasn't. So I walked to her house. She saw me coming. Met me at the door. Pulled me in and enveloped me in her arms. Then wisely she waited for me to tell her what I wanted. She, at that time, lived with her sister, Estella Marsh. Upon hearing the purpose of my visit, we kneeled. They both laid their hands on me and prayed. Even as I write this, I can feel the power of that day. Their strong hands on my head and back. Their prayers full of love, wisdom, and understanding. I knew that regardless of how hard the year's studies were, I could make it now. And I did. For God really and truly answered their prayers that day.

Her prayers not only made a difference while she lived, they still make a difference today. Her niece, Sue, writing from a hospital bed, recalled times she had called Aunt Cecil in the middle of the night. It was 3:00 a.m. in a hospital in Washington D.C. She was facing a very complex surgical procedure. Without surgery, complete paralysis. With surgery, possible complete paralysis. A phone call and Aunt Cecil was on the line talking, advising, calming fears and praying. The surgery results? Complete recovery.

But perhaps one of the most outstanding stories to come out of this quest for ways Aunt Cecil made a difference in the lives she touched comes from a soldier. He says:

"In order to appreciate this memory, you will have to put yourself inside the body of a First Lieutenant and feel the mixed emotions, fears, anxiety and even constant nausea he experiences just twenty-four hours before leaving for overseas duty and battle. You see, I was an officer, an infantry officer at that. I could not let anyone see my tears, so I cried at night in those lonesome hours. By doing this I even concealed my feelings from my wife.

"We were visiting my parents the afternoon before leaving for combat. I packed all my belongings except my knife which I took outside and sharpened as I sat at the picnic table. Dad walked up. Sat down. Watched. After a long silence (Remember, he was a Quaker. They are noted for their peace loving and anti-war stands.), Dad spoke quietly, 'Son, I hope you never have to use that.' With that remark, I almost lost all . . . all those secrets I had hidden inside me, what I knew I was facing, how I had been trained, and what I was prepared to do. I got up and I guess you would say I escaped.

"I got in my car with no place to go and took off. I drove around town, up and down the main street, Harrison. Then I thought of Aunt Cecil and how strong she always appeared to be. I wondered just how she would react if she were me. I went to her house. Knocked on the door. She came from the kitchen and before she even got to the door, she said, 'I was just praying for you.'

"She opened the door and embraced me in two of the strongest arms I ever felt. We sat and she cried, something I wanted to do so badly. With her gentle and wise insight, she expressed the very feelings I was having at that time. Reaching for her Bible, she read a passage, closed the Bible and prayed. Now, when Aunt Cecil prayed, it was not just mere words. She placed those long, strong, loving arms around me and began reminding God of Daniel and the lion's den, about Moses and the Red Sea, and of David and Goliath. Then she simply asked for God's protection and my safe return. All of heaven seemed to descend. I was completely wrapped in God's love and hers. Strengthened, if you please, to go out and face the enemy. And fight for my country. And protect those I love.

"Encouraged, renewed, restrengthened, and empowered,

I got up, told her good-bye, and left. As I drove away, I turned and looked back one more time. There she stood. Open Bible in one hand and waving good-bye with the other.

"I will never forget those arms embracing me and then waving good-bye. God must have made those arms appear strong that day. For you see, one night during a heated battle, I saw those arms and once again received strength.

"Was it Aunt Cecil's prayers which caused me to move quickly to another foxhole when two of us dived into the same one? Minutes later the foxhole I had just vacated blew up. The far-reaching effects of her prayers were felt there on the battlefield that dark night. They are still being felt today. Her prayers made a difference."

Cancer claimed her life at age eighty-six on September 19, 1980, six weeks after surgery revealed it. The arthritis under her rib cage she often referred to was not arthritis, but the more dreaded pain of a fatal disease.

People from all walks of life with all levels of education came to pay her tribute when she died. Listen to excerpts from the eulogy which was read at her funeral held in the little Quaker Church in Alexandria, Indiana, where she was a charter member:

> In all our lives there exists that one object, that one place or that one person from whom we receive solace. This solace might range from Pike's Peak to the Chesapeake Bay. From the Gulf of Mexico to the Arctic Sea. Aunt Cecil was that solace to many of us. She always listened. Always understood. Was the first to assist in whatever trial or tribulation one might have.
>
> . . .Presidents have died with amassed fortunes at their feet. Aunt Cecil lies here today with no earthly fortune, but life eternal. As we look back upon the life of this Christian soldier, we find that by a simple telephone call, she was able to give encouragement to those who sought. Friendship to those who wrote. And stability to those who visited. She represents a Sunday school teacher, church member, church advisor, preacher, song evangelist, counselor and prayer warrior.
>
> . . .Man erects Halls of Fame for outstanding football, baseball, and basketball stars. We build libraries as monuments to commemorate our presidents. Well, there won't be any Hall of Fame or library as a monument to Aunt Cecil. Basically, this would be anti-climactic. For God has prepared a mansion in heaven for her.

Aunt Cecil saw wrong and prayed for it to be righted. She observed violence and prayed for it to cease. She felt discomfort and prayed for its healing. She touched lives by merely being a shepherd. We can all remember Aunt Cecil looking upward and singing, "Follow, I Will Follow Thee, My Lord" and "It Is Well With My Soul."

Aunt Cecil, you have been a warrior, a model, a saint, an inspiration and an institution. Thank you. We love you.

Saints? What do you think of when you hear the word? What do they look like? For many of us, the answer is "Aunt Cecil."

Ruth Kelley Argo

by Marie Evatt

I consecrated you as an infant to be a missionary to Africa" was the joyful response of Ruth Kelley's godly mother when she first heard about her daughter's call to missionary service.

On a cold January day in South Carolina, a sparkling brown-eyed baby girl was born into the home of Reverend and Mrs. Lawrence H. Kelley. Baby Ruth brought special warmth into that home, not only as a child, but also in her teen and adult years as she gave her heart to the Lord and began proving "that good, and acceptable, and perfect will of God" for her life.

Four brothers and two sisters completed the family circle. Concerned that their family be in a Christian environment, Mr. and Mrs. Kelley moved to Central, South Carolina, where their children could attend Central Wesleyan College.

Ruth was an active, wide-awake young lady, making many friends and entering wholeheartedly into many school activities. At age 16, she was soundly converted. People noticed a decided change in her life. A year later, at the altar of Central Wesleyan College, she was sanctified. Since then the pursuit of godliness has been her goal! Jesus Christ has been her model! During her college years, concern for the spiritual welfare of her friends was evident. Perhaps the Lord was beginning to answer the dedicatory prayer and commitment of her godly parents.

Ruth remembers this period in her life as a time when she was surrounded by the love and prayers of her parents,

83

enjoyed the companionship of a devoted Christian girl friend, and sensed the compassion and tenderness of her pastor. Dedicated, Christian faculty members, students with Christ-centered goals, consistent adults of the local church and a conference (district) that filled its camp meeting pulpit with outstanding, godly evangelists were other significant influences in Ruth's Christian growth and development.

During a Greer (South Carolina) camp meeting service, Ruth felt led to go to Asbury College in Wilmore, Kentucky for her senior year of college. Faithfully she attended the class prayer meetings, the monthly on-campus missionary meetings, and the Wilmore Methodist church.

One Sunday afternoon in the college chapel, during an electrifying missionary service, this attractive Southern belle felt inclined to respond to the missionary speaker's invitation for those willing to offer themselves for missionary service to come forward and kneel at the chapel altar. Was this really from the Lord she wondered? Or was it just a response to the feeling generated by an emotionally-packed service? Fearing it was the latter, Ruth did not go forward.

Sunday evening found her again at the Methodist church. There was no question about it. God was speaking to her. The Holy Spirit followed her to her dormitory room and manifested himself in such a marked way that Ruth knew God was calling her to serve Him in Africa. As Isaiah of old, she responded: "Here am I, send me."

Ruth wrote to her mother immediately. Her mother joyfully reminded her that she had been consecrated as an infant to be a missionary to Africa!"

After her 1929 graduation from Asbury College, she returned to Central, South Carolina, and became active in the life of the Second Wesleyan Church while teaching in a nearby community school and later at Central College. I was a member of the pre-school "card" class taught by this lovely brunette whose very life radiated the principles of holy, godly living. Not only was she my Sunday school teacher, she assisted with YMWB and helped to direct public children's programs. Under her loving direction, I remember saying my first lines in public – often these were scripture verses. Memorization of Psalm 100 dates back to those days.

The rules of the contest are now very foggy, but I do remember that sometime during the years I was in her "card" class, Ruth gave me a little New Testament for having "met all the requirements!" I was receiving wonderful Christian

84

training in my home; my father read to us twice daily from the Word. But those were the depression years so I had no Bible of my own until Ruth gave me that little New Testament. What a prize! What a treasure! That New Testament is still tucked away in my South Carolina home. It means a great deal to me. Not only is it God's Word, it represents a lady whom I've known since childhood who has "wholly followed the Lord".

Her friends and family watched her and speculated about her future. Would Ruth settle down to teaching and forget her call to Africa? During those years at Central College, a serious-minded student caught Ruth's eye. Archie J. Argo and Ruth Kelley could often be seen enjoying each other's company. Now there were two hurdles to cross – a stateside teaching profession and an admiring young man.

In 1936, Ruth was given the opportunity to go to Sierra Leone, West Africa. Would she go? Of course. She never waivered in answering God's call to overseas service. Who accompanied her to the train for a last good-bye? Archie J. Argo!

Ruth herself best summarizes her dedication and devotion to the Lord and His call in her farewell message found in *The Wesleyan Missionary,* October 1936.

> "It was seven years ago when the Holy Spirit spoke clearly to me about my taking the place of Sister Cleo Clement in Africa. Since that time, I have been working and making plans to answer that call. I feel grateful to God and the Church that the time has now come for me to take up my work in that dark continent. Viewing it from a human standpoint, the task is great. But I am going in the name of Him who gave the command, 'Go.' The promises of the Bible do not fail. I have the blessed assurance that He will go with me. That thought calms my fears, strengthens my faith, and encourages my heart.
>
> "As I leave the homeland, it is a source of encouragement to know that the Church will be praying for me. I am wholly yielded to the Lord and my prayer is that souls will be saved and sanctified in the work to which I have been entrusted."

For the next three years, Ruth lived in Kamabai and served as principal or headmistress of Clarke Memorial Girl's School, at that time the only school for girls located in the Northern Province, Sierra Leone, West Africa. During those years she realized the importance of knowing that God had called her to Africa. It was not easy to be separated from home, friends, and a sweetheart! However, the joy of the Lord was her strength so she found it a delight to work with the girls in the school.

The girls' school did not claim all of Ruth's time and concern. Shortly after her arrival, she visited Kamakwie, the medical center of Wesleyan missions in Sierra Leone. There she saw physical suffering being relieved as well as the way of salvation being taught.

A visit to Kunso, the first Wesleyan mission station, was on the itinerary of one early Sierra Leone trek. Ruth stated that when walking through the Kunso cemetery, she felt she was walking on the most holy ground on which she had ever walked. Nine graves located beneath the African palms represented young people, including one child, who gave their lives so that Sierra Leoneans might be among the Lord's redeemed.

Ruth was known as a missionary who did not allow pressing duties to keep her from communion with God. The discipline of a regular quiet time with her Lord has continued to this very day. When Ruth prays, one senses being in the presence of one who communes as easily with the Lord as with an earthly friend.

October 27, 1938, marked Ruth's safe arrival in the New York harbor after an Atlantic voyage which began in Freetown on September 21. As her boat had pulled away from Freetown, along with twelve others, two destroyers and an airplane were searching the area for German submarines! The journey home was not without its dangers, but Ruth's promise was: "The angel of the Lord encampeth round about them that fear him, and delivereth them" (Psalm 34:7). Who was there to greet Ruth when she arrived? None other than the admirer who had said good-bye three years earlier!

Deputation responsibilities claimed the attention of this furloughing missionary. Many wonderful people became Ruth's friends as a result of these missionary services but one friend continued to be the most loved and admired of all. On September 7, 1940, Ruth Kelley became the loving bride of the Reverend Archie J. Argo.

As a teenager of 15 years, I was delighted to see my former Sunday school teacher who had become a real live missionary happily married. My impression of all that had happened and was happening in Ruth's life can be summarized in the words of Jesus "Seek ye first the kingdom of God, and his righteousness; and all these things shall be added unto you" (Matthew 6:33).

Archie and Ruth spent the first years of their married life

86

serving in pastoral and teaching ministries. During my college years, I was greatly influenced by this dedicated couple, both in the classroom and on the campus. I will never forget their deep commitment to Christ and to each other.

Friends wondered and questioned. Would Ruth ever get back to the mission field? In 1944 the missions board asked Archie and Ruth Argo to go to Sierra Leone and be the first resident missionaries in Susu land. The Susu people were staunch Moslems so this would not be an easy task. Their answer was an obedient yes.

The trip to Sierra Leone — Archie's first, Ruth's second — was an eventful one. Leaving Miami, Florida, on May 8, 1944, their journey took them via Cuba to Port-au-Prince (Haiti), to San Juan (Puerto Rico), to Port of Spain (Trinidad), to Georgetown (Guyana), to Belem and Natal (Brazil) to Liberia (Africa) and then to Sierra Leone arriving in Sulima on June 9. Traveling cross-country, they arrived at our Wesleyan work on June 12, thirty-five days after leaving Miami! (What a contrast to my last trip to Sierra Leone when I left my home in South Carolina on a Saturday and ate Sunday dinner with missionaries at our Freetown rest house.)

Pioneering in Susu land was not easy. The people responded well and appreciated the medical and educational ministries but their interest and allegiance to the message of Jesus Christ was almost nil. On one occasion Ruth wrote:

> "We are not smitten by the Amalekites, but we find as we labor among a Mohammedan people that we, like David, must encourage ourselves in the Lord. The promises of our Jehovah bring new courage to us, and we shall continue to cry unto Him day and night until this people is awakened to their need of Jesus Christ as a Savior" (*The Wesleyan Missionary,* Nov. 1945).

The Tonko Limba chiefdom bordered Susu country. Ruth ministered in their villages and found the Tonko Limbas' response to the gospel encouraging and rewarding.

The years whisked by. Furlough time arrived. The Argos had courageously witnessed to the Susus, the Tonko Limbas, as well as to other tribes. It was time to wend their way homeward and share with those of us waiting anxiously to hear about their adventures for the Lord.

Shortly after their return to the states in 1947, Ruth added a new dimension to her life — another of those "all things" that was added because she sought first God's kingdom. On July 29, Ruth became the mother of David Argo and on December 1, 1948, Paul Edward Argo was born. Because of the birth of these two sons, the Argos were in the states for longer than a one-year furlough.

During the latter part of 1948, doors began opening for me to answer God's call to missionary service. I was 23; and for my mother, that seemed very young for her last-born child to be going alone and so far away from home. Fortunately, Ruth Argo and her family were living in Central, South Carolina, at that time. Ruth was a source of inspiration and courage for both me and my mother. She told me what to take and what not to take, what to expect, etc., etc.

In God's kind providence, I accompanied the Argos to Sierra Leone. My mother willingly placed me in their loving care, and they graciously "adopted"' this first-term missionary along with their two young sons. During my first term, I knew I had a trusted friend in Ruth Argo. She continued to be the example of faithfulness, courage and godliness that I had observed as a child in her "card" class. Ruth and Archie lived in Binkolo that term, serving as mission coordinator and mission hostess. Ruth cared for the children and kept the mission books while Pa Argo, along with Conference President Brahama Turay, traveled from church to church.

That term passed quickly. Ruth and Archie returned for furlough in 1952, fully expecting to return to Sierra Leone the next year. God had other plans.

Paul, their second son, became ill. The Argo family terminated overseas service and began pastoring in North Carolina. Their submissive, obedient spirits exemplified a continued willingness for the Lord's will to be their will.

Thirteen years of pastoral ministry followed, three at King's Mountain and ten at High Point, Hayworth Memorial. At the beginning of their eleventh year as pastor of the Hayworth church, Rev. Argo suffered a massive heart attack and died suddenly.

This was not the first tragedy that Ruth had faced. During her first year after college, her father, the Reverend L. H. Kelley, and twenty-two-year-old brother had been killed in a car and train accident near Central. Ruth had learned to face adversity with courage; her faith in God never waivered.

Ruth, now widowed, was comforted in knowing that God would not forsake her and her two teenage sons. Ruth describes the next four years as years of anxiety, though she never showed this to others, as she taught at Kernersville Wesleyan Academy and cared for her afflicted son, Paul.

On December 3, 1970, Jesus chose to heal Paul by taking

him Home. Ruth again committed what she could not understand to the Lord and prayed: "Not my will but thine be done." With confidence that God does all things well, Ruth found peace. Those of us who observed her during those days were aware that her foundation was solid. She had a faith that would not shrink. Through all of these tragedies and adversities, Ruth's life proved true God's Word which says:

> "When thou passest through the waters, I will be with thee; and through the rivers, they shall not overflow thee: When thou walkest through the fire, thou shalt not be burned; neither shall the flame kindle upon thee. For I am the Lord thy God, the Holy One of Israel, thy Saviour . . . Fear not: for I am with thee" (Isaiah 43:2, 3a, 5a).

The early 1970s again showed "the stuff" out of which Ruth is made. She returned to the Hayworth church as assistant to the pastor. Included in this were visiting, teaching a Sunday school class, coaching a youth Bible bowl team, leading prayer groups and serving wherever needed. Her older son, David, was by now a minister in the United Methodist Church.

In 1975, Ruth returned to Central, South Carolina, to live near her aged mother, known to many of us as Sister Emma. Teaching a Sunday school class, coaching Bible Bowl teams, serving as lay leader of Trinity Wesleyan Church, until recently working part-time in the library of Central Wesleyan College, walking several miles in the early morning, sharing her home with guests who need either a place for overnight or a longer period of time, praying earnestly for family, friends and overseas missionary work are among Ruth's current activities.

In finding Christ and utterly abandoning herself to Him and His will for her life, Ruth Kelley Argo found herself and knew she was a "somebody," a child of the Heavenly King. Having total confidence in Ruth's faith and knowing how her life had intertwined with mine, I asked Ruth Kelley Argo to participate in my 1981 installation as general director of Wesleyan Women International (formerly, Wesleyan Women's Missionary Society).

Many mental pictures flash before me as I think about this outstanding lady. One act demonstrates her character. *The setting:* Greer camp meeting. *The time:* offering appeal. *The opportunity:* Money she had saved to buy a washing machine. *The decision:* Prompted by the Holy Spirit, she gave her washing machine money to help finance Greer camp meeting. That incident is characteristic of Ruth's lifestyle of obedience. Since her conversion at age 16, she has been "a living sacrifice, holy, acceptable unto God."

Ruth Senison Liddick

by Olive Coleson

As she pulled the pancake turner from the drawer, something moved! She reached a hand to investigate, then snatched it back. A snake was coiled there expectantly.

She called her husband and together they killed the two-and-a-half-foot poisonous viper.

A bit shaken, but undaunted, they finished breakfast and sat down to praise the Lord once more for His protection. It was just one of the many things she had committed to Him long ago.

It all started when baby Ruth was born to Harry and Jennie P. Sension on June 22, 1906 in Philadelphia, Pennsylvania. She was the eleventh child of twelve and like the others she was dedicated to the Lord.

Ruth was saved at age six and became a soul winner right away. She crawled up on her beloved father's knee and asked him to let Jesus come into his heart. Later she invited a Catholic man to a camp meeting where he was converted. She attended the Nazarene church with her family and often visited a Christian mission with her sister, Naomi, on Sunday afternoons. The pastor taught scripture memorization and witnessing and invited them to sing and witness at the rescue missions where he ministered.

High school brought testing times. Ruth's goal, to prepare for missionary service, was not understood by many of her classmates. The 1924 yearbook listed her "Last Will and Testament" as follows: "Name, Ruth Sension; Characteristic, silence; Favorite Fad, church; Ambition, to convert cannibals." They obviously knew where she stood! Later, one of her classmates found Christ and became a missionary to Africa.

After graduation she attended Nyack Missionary Training Institute for two years. She applied for service in India, but when there was no opening, she enrolled at Booth Memorial Hospital in New York City with Nyack classmates for nurses' training.

After her father's sudden death, she returned to Philadelphia, enrolled at the Episcopal Hospital, and became a registered nurse. While there she attended a nearby Wesleyan church and soon became leader of its youth group.

Here she met her future husband, Alton Liddick, a handsome musically talented young man. They organized a five-member string band and traveled all over the district singing and witnessing. These two promising youths were delegates to the first National Youth Conference held in Houghton, New York.

Ruth's mother, a warm-hearted, devoted Christian, had a burden for the lost. She must have prayed the need of "Go ye" into her offspring. Four of her children and three grandchildren became missionaries. What a legacy! In 1932, her mother was hospitalized and Ruth cared for her until she went to be with the Lord.

That same summer President James Luckey was traveling to the churches looking for a nurse for Houghton College. Although Ruth was not present when he visited the Philadelphia church, the people told him about her. Soon Ruth had a call from Dr. Luckey and responded to the need in the fall of 1932, serving in the college infirmary while she attended her freshman year at the college.

On July 1, 1933, Ruth and Alton were joined in marriage in the Philadelphia church. Immediately after Professor Frank Wright finished the ceremony, the couple set out for Houghton College to prepare more fully for India while Ruth continued her work as college nurse.

Exciting news soon followed. Dr. E. F. McCarty, Secretary of Wesleyan World Missions, asked if they would consider going to India in the fall. This was the opportunity they had been waiting for! They terminated school that spring and began to prepare for departure.

It was a day of rejoicing when they boarded the ship for India. They faced the unknown future with confidence, because they were responding to God's call.

After the long, tiring trip from New York to Bombay, it

.was a relief to travel overland by train to Sanjan, about one hundred miles north. There they were warmly greeted by missionaries and a group of eager Indian Christians who placed bright flower garlands about their necks to welcome them.

The Sanjan mission station, complete with a bungalow, church and dispensary, was just a short distance from the railway station. The Liddicks were stationed there while beginning to study the Gujerati language.

Bursting with eagerness to start giving out the Good News of the gospel, they found they must sit with a teacher for many hours a day and later go to language school for three months at the hill station. One-and-a-half years of intense study were required. They worked diligently and succeeded, also becoming well-versed in Indian culture.

They labored largely among Hindus, a very religious people having millions of gods. The caste system was a distinct barrier to Christianity.

Their aim was threefold: to evangelize, to develop the national church and train local ministers, and to turn the work over to competent national leaders.

Life in India was a challenge. The Liddicks learned to sleep under mosquito nets, boil all drinking water, soak fresh vegetables in saline or chlorine solutions, then rinse them in boiled water to protect their health.

The refrigerator ran on kerosene, if available. The Indians were puzzled about how a light burning under it could produce ice.

The burning heat of the sun, the hot dust of the dry season and the humid, moldy rainy season summoned all the ingenuity they could muster. There were no air-conditioners or electric fans in the jungle!

Water had to be carried from the well. Candles and kerosene lanterns provided light to study that strange language.

Transportation was by foot, bullock cart, cycle, and train. Ruth occasionally traveled by cycle while serving as a nurse in the Sanjan and Dhagadmar dispensaries. She also ministered with her Bible women in the surrounding villages and conducted children's meetings, teaching the boys and girls to play in a rhythm band.

Ruth didn't exactly relish the daily battle against bugs, insects, scorpions, and snakes. But she often sensed God's miraculous deliverance.

"A few hours after our arrival home from vacation," she

93

remembers, "I opened a hall closet and lifted out a pile of small rugs. When I lifted them a few minutes later, a three-foot-long cobra slid from the middle of the rugs. I dropped the whole pile and the snake slithered across the bed and on to the floor. It was as frightened as I was and continued to slither back and forth wildly under the bed. I called for help and our house girl came running with two canes. After a battle she gave the final blow that killed the snake. I thanked the Lord for His protection."

India has been called the world's main reservoir of infection for plague, cholera, smallpox, and malaria. Leprosy is also prevalent. Sickness is mostly attributed to evil spirits. Fearing the evil eye, Indians wear charms hoping to keep it away. They believe that their gods, when displeased, visit them with sickness and disease.

Ruth's nurses' training was certainly planned of God.

Vera Clocksen wrote, "I witnessed firsthand her wise and gentle dealings with the Indian people. She was careful to observe their customs when appropriate, so as not to offend them. She had good rapport with them and was well respected."

Chotalal B. Christian recalled, "In March 1948 twins were born in my family. I was passing through financial difficulties at the time of their birth. Mrs. Liddick helped my sons by providing powdered milk and nursing care for two years. It was very valuable. I thank the Lord for inspiring her to help me."

Two children were born to Ruth and Alton in India. Edith Jean, born in February 1937, lived only five days.

Hazel Jones remembers, "When Edith Jean was born and lived for such a short time, I marveled at Ruth's fortitude. As she pressed the last kiss on that beautiful baby face, there was just calm confidence that her loving Heavenly Father doeth all things well."

Dean Alton was born on February 27, 1939. Louise Lytle reported, "His birth was very precarious. At Brooksville, Ruth recounted in a devotional how she traveled by stretcher and train to the distant hospital."

Hazel Jones continued, "Ruth had a steadfast trust in God as Dean hovered between life and death. Ruth's enduring faith encouraged the father and nurse as they walked the floors with a darling, suffering baby. It was a heavenly atmosphere when the Lord manifested His presence with miracles that made little Dean a normal, mischievous infant. I, the nurse, stood beside

Ruth as we gazed at a healthy boy taking his nap. Tears ran down our faces as we thanked the Lord."

Before returning to America, Ruth wrote of *Deliverance by Delay*. "In 1940 land had been purchased for a farm colony and it was voted to build a mission bungalow there.

"The hot season settled in before building permits were granted. So Alton and Floyd Banker stayed to complete the bungalow, while I took Baby Dean a thousand miles to the Hill Station in the northern Himalaya Mountains.

"Six weeks later they made reservations on the Frontier Mail, a daily express train to the north.

"When the travel day was near, they realized the roof could not be finished. The building must be roofed before the rainy season, but Ruth and others in the hills had no way of knowing of the change.

"On the day of their expected arrival, word came that the Frontier Mail train had been wrecked. Since they were traveling one day later and we did not know that, we waited in vain. You can understand our great concern. The news told that an Englishman had been killed, and our men would have been traveling in the same car with him. But there was no news of them.

"During those twenty-four hours of waiting, I know that I fit into the title of one of the Sunday school lessons, 'Here am I, God, worries and all!' But there was a permeating peace as well as much prayer.

"A missionary friend of the Free Methodist Church came to comfort us. He said that since Floyd and Alton carried self-identification papers, they would have been included in the list of victims – dead or injured.

"And so we prayed on as we waited. When they arrived safely, we understood the delay. God's protective hand had been at work. Just one more day to finish the roof had saved their lives. The Lord's blessings are new every day."

Due to World War II the Liddicks had an extended furlough and traveled thousands of miles in deputation. They were both gifted speakers.

Vera Clocksen Schrag states: "She was the speaker for our Foreign Missionary Fellowship at Houghton College. I was impressed with her enthusiasm and dedication. She was a convincing speaker, making the work of His Kingdom attractive and impressive."

Ruth told me about their return to India for a second term. "During World War II in 1945," she said, "we returned

95

to India with sixty other missionaries. Traveling under convoy of forty-five ships, we arrived in Egypt and had to disembark. Our embassy sent us by train to another port to await passage to Bombay, India.

"Needing to cash travelers' checks, we went to a bank in Port Said. Starting back toward the railway station, we realized we had left our briefcase. Quickly returning we saw it near the teller's window, but the bank had closed.

"We were stunned momentarily, but called upon the Lord for help. Just then an Egyptian approached us and asked why we were staring through the bank window. When we pointed to the briefcase, he produced the key, unlocked the door and gave us the briefcase. He was the bank watchman.

"We thanked him and the Lord. Rushing back to the railroad station, we found some missionaries frantically looking for us while others were delaying the train!

"What a remarkable answer to prayer in a strange land!"

Arriving in India for the second time, they were stationed at the newly settled farm colony of Dhagadmar. This term was to be filled with important meetings with Indian officials, building projects at Dhagadmar and Pardi, dispensary and evangelistic work, plus countless hours of prayer and counseling.

Another of their responsibilities was to welcome new missionaries. On October 29, 1946, my husband, Ralph, and I and our baby, Dorothy, arrived in India. Rev. Liddick helped us buy supplies and traveled with us up-country by train.

Since we couldn't speak the language and didn't understand Indian customs, we spent our first months with the Liddicks before leaving for language school in the mountains.

My first meeting with Ruth stands out vividly in my memory. What a joy it was to be met by this petite lady with open arms and a warm heart! Hopping along beside her was eight-year-old Dean, curious to see what his new friend would look like. Hoping to have a real playmate, he was astonished to see a nine-week-old baby and exclaimed, "My, is she a midget?"

Ruth invited us into her cozy mission bungalow. She was a gracious hostess and a good cook, so we were quickly shown to our bedroom and nearby bath to freshen up after India's dusty roads.

I remember the chicken dinner and ice cream for dessert we enjoyed that day in HOT India! We thought we'd said good-bye to that treat for six-and-a-half years. To be sure, it was a delicacy! Kerosene was rationed, but they'd obtained a small amount to put in their tiny refrigerator, which made

nine ice cubes or five small servings of ice cream. We slowly
savored each bite!

As we enjoyed getting acquainted over the candlelight dinner, I noticed a motto hanging on the wall: "Not somehow,
but triumphantly." As I came to know this couple, I realized
that this motto not only adorned their home but their hearts
as well.

To take another family of three into their small two-bed-
room, one-bath bungalow for three to four months was a sacrifice they made – not somehow, but triumphantly – as to Jesus
himself.

Dean's schoolroom became our bedroom. Having a baby
around wasn't what he'd expected, but I never heard him complain.

What a privilege to be introduced to India by this close-
knit, loving family. As Dorothy grew older, she and Dean had
lots of fun together. There were hard lessons and hours of
learning, but there were also times of good fellowship, picnics,
and many wonderful outings.

We learned we were "but'chas" (beginners). Not only did
we study language, but we tried to learn how India thinks,
talks, and acts. Soon we were winding our tongues around a
new alphabet: the "k" followed by its aspirated "kh," the "g"
followed by "gh," and so on.

On our first Sunday morning Ruth had the Indian Christians sing an original welcome song in English for us. I will
never forget the refrain: "India needs you, India needs you
. . .," over and over again.

Vera Clocksen said, "Ruth's great sense of humor carried
her through many a difficult situation which made life enjoy-
able even when much was to the contrary. She added much
spice to our station meetings and get-togethers."

Sunday afternoons we had English Sunday school for Dean
because he didn't understand the Indian service. We sang children's songs, gave children's lessons, memorized scripture verses, and listened to simple testimonies.

The Liddicks were both gifted musicians. They sang well,
played the piano and other instruments, and taught Dean to
sing. Their family theme song was "He Signed the Deed."

We shared family devotions with them daily. Before starting on a trip, we always stopped under a tree and prayed for
traveling mercies.

We learned many things that helped us in our serving
as we watched Indian ways. We talked over missionary prob-

lems, deputation travels, national workers, and the state of the church and nation with the Liddicks.

Ruth taught me to plan carefully. Food was rationed. Flour was scarce and often full of bugs. We learned to sift and use it anyway. Food was stored in tight tins or sealed in jars to keep the bugs out until it was used.

We had no refrigeration for two years so we cooked only what we could eat each day. Snakebite and scorpion sting medications were kept ready for use. Drinking water was strained, boiled, and cooled in earthen jugs. These were precautions to protect our health.

These details of life were important to remember, but I learned much greater lessons from Ruth. I observed her commitment to God's will in the sorrows as well as the joys of life. When lonely for family in America, she handled it with letters and prayers.

When health problems and death of loved ones back in the States came along, she testified: "There was no plane service and no money. How could one leave his own family for so long a time? We knew that was part of the sacrifice in the 'Go ye.' Alton's parents both died during our first term. But, oh, the peace that Jesus gives! In such times as these, we had it."

When her husband became Foreign Missionary Secretary in the States, she was the ideal helpmeet. For fourteen years Ruth served as secretary in the Department of World Missions. She enjoyed traveling to mission fields with her husband whenever possible (at her own expense). She wrote two booklets for the mission department: *A Great Door and Effectual Is Opened*" and "*Fifty Years in India.*"

During their retirement years in Brooksville, Florida, Louise Lytle observed, "They lived for each other and basked in their home, yard, and Bible study. Seeing his health weakening, they sold their home and moved into a small apartment which Ruth can occupy as long as she needs it."

"They had daily intercessory prayer together reaching around the world. Ruth gave Alton constant nursing care for many months. But, shut in with God, they still carried on His ministry.

"We wondered how Ruth would cope after Alton's death," Mrs. Lytle continued, "but she has made a wonderful adjustment. She is always bright and cheerful and often greets one with a joke. She attends services, is active in the Wednesday prayer meetings, and takes her turn at playing the piano or leading devotions.

"Ruth learned to drive after she turned fifty. What a blessing that she is able to drive to the hospital, the dentist, and the grocery store. Her son, Dean, is a constant source of encouragement to her."

In 1985 after Alton's death she wrote, "I live, watch, wait, and occupy in anticipation of the Rapture. Today? Perhaps! Maranatha!"

My life has been greatly influenced by this woman of God who, like Ruth of the Bible, dared to leave all for Him.

She carefully prepared to serve her Master, never losing sight of her goal.

She trusted the Lord for a companion. God sent His choice for her. Together they conquered the difficult language barrier, adapted to life in a hot climate, experienced miracles of God's wonderful care in many circumstances, and best of all, saw lives transformed and a church established in India.

She had a radiance on her face and a reservoir of strength from her Lord: as she cared for her mother in her last illness; as she kissed sweet Edith Jean good-bye; as she hovered over her afflicted son until healing came; as she loved and served her beloved until she laid him in the arms of Jesus.

"Not somehow, but triumphantly!"

Epilogue

"Let her own works praise her" (Proverbs 31:31).

"The key word that best describes Ruth is devotion: first to the Lord, and then to her family."

–Gracia Fero Banker, editor
The Wesleyan Missionary
Missionary to Jamaica

"Ruth was a faithful wife, a thankful mother, an ideal homemaker and hostess."

–Hazel Jones, coworker
Retired missionary to India

"Ruth's bright, chipper spirit is an inspiration to those who know her."

—Louise Lytle
Missionary to Colombia
Wife of Alton's assistant in
Wesleyan World Missions

"She is very witty, outgoing, cheerful, creative with her typewriter and greeting cards."

—Maude Higgins, fellow nurse
Houghton College

"My boss's wife. She never let the office girls feel she was different. Unchangeable. True friend."

—Genevieve Dick Pinkerton
Secretary in missions office

"When my mother was critically ill, Ruth personally visited her. This meant much to me."

—Margaret Wright
Missionary to India & Nepal

"Ruth was a careful shopper, such a pleasant person to wait on. We shared the same first name and birthdate."

—Ruth Barker, grocery clerk
Houghton, New York

"A woman of prayer. We enjoyed the beautifully served teas she provided for her friends."

—Helen Paine, president's wife
Houghton College

"I have always admired Mrs. Liddick as a gracious person and competent nurse, mother, and wife."

—Ruth Fancher Hutton
Houghton College faculty member

Myrtle Carter

by JoAnne Lyon

Myrtle Carter held her beautiful two-year-old lifeless baby in her arms and cried, "Oh God, take me, too." For the first time in her life she called out to God, and He answered her: "You can't go where she's going."

Myrtle wasn't sure what this meant, but somehow she knew there had to be an answer. After the funeral and burial arrangements were over, Myrtle continued to hear those words, "You can't go where she's going," over and over in her mind.

In this small eastern Kansas town a Christian couple endured ridicule from many of their neighbors, including Myrtle. But as she reflected on the criticism, she came to the conclusion that these were the very people who could help her. She quickly made her way down the dusty road to the home of the Raineys. As Mrs. Rainey invited her in, Myrtle simply blurted out, "Can you help me find God?" The Raineys were the "saints" of the community and knew exactly how to fulfill the request. They belonged to a small holiness church and could "pray the glory down." In a few minutes this same fire of forgiveness and hope hit Myrtle and she shouted all over their house, praising God for His mercy.

On the way home she could not keep quiet. She stopped along the way and told neighbors of her newly found faith. She knew her husband, Clyde, would be thrilled to hear the good news. When he swept through the door that night, she eagerly reported the life-changing event of the day. About midway through, he interrupted her. "Myrtle, I don't want to hear any more. This is the worst thing you could have done. You've

103

ruined me, my family, and my name. Now you get hold of yourself and forget all about this religion stuff, and I mean *now.*"

Myrtle was stunned. The next morning, as soon as Clyde left for work, she rushed down to the Raineys. Their lack of surprise at Clyde's response was reassuring to her and somehow after their prayer, she knew she could not give up her faith.

The times of Bible study and prayers with the Raineys continued to strengthen her, and at the same time her larger extended family increasingly rejected her.

One day Clyde announced they were selling out and moving to Texas to make their fortune in the oil boom. "Myrtle," he thundered, "get all this stuff ready and the two kids and let's get out of Longton." This order was met with ambivalence on Myrtle's part. She was definitely glad to get out of Longton – the small, gossipy town, but she surmised that the rough oil boom town of Texas – living in a tent – was no place to raise children and no place for a Christian lady.

However, she had now learned to take her questions, concerns, and cares to the Lord. Bidding her extended family good-bye was difficult. She longed that they might come to know the Lord as she did. She had tried to share her faith with them many times, but it had fallen on deaf ears. Now she was moving far away and saw no hope of their conversion.

She had not yet learned how God weaves all the events in our lives into a beautiful tapestry. But she was beginning.

. . .

Arriving at the "boom town," she realized her need to pray for God to open other doors. This was her first solo adventure in the field of prayer, far apart from her mentors in Longton.

She had learned well. Within a few weeks Clyde came home with an unusual amount of energy. He lightly touched the children on the head as he made for the kitchen. "Myrtle," he said with a lift to his voice. She whirled around with pie dough on her hands, for she had never heard this much excitement and joy come from him. "I have a job with the Continental Oil Company in Wichita, Kansas. We can move right now."

Myrtle was not sure which miracle was the greatest – the job or answered prayer!

She quickly gathered their few material things into the Model A and they made their way north, through Oklahoma, then only a few years removed from Indian territory. Clyde reminisced about the time he was placed in the back of a covered wagon at the age of two and told to hold on tight. The government had set aside that day for the remainder of the land in Oklahoma known as the "Cherokee Strip" to be settled. His father had gone ahead on a mule and staked out the land. His mother put the two children in the wagon and lined up along with the rest of the land hopefuls. When the guns exploded, they took off as fast as the horses could take them to claim their fortune. Clyde chuckled, "This is good land. Mom and Dad could have made a fortune in this oil down here, but they got homesick for Longton. Soon they sold their land and moved back to Longton. I guess friends and family were more important to them than fortune." As they jostled on through Oklahoma, Myrtle thought about the little home she could fix comfortably for her family. Her nimble fingers could construct colorful skirts out of feed sacks around the orange crates for all kinds of tables. The children tried to imagine their new school. What would they do in such a large city?

Those thoughts on that dry, rutted road soon became reality. Myrtle found a little church down the street from their rented bungalow and became a regular attender. The singing and preaching spoke to her heart. The people welcomed her as one of their family. But Clyde became jealous. He started getting drunk on Saturday nights and came home in a drunken stupor. About 4:00 a.m. he began vomiting. Myrtle would spend hours cleaning up the mess. However, it never detoured her from church. Clyde's hours became later and later. He then started accusing her of being in love with the preacher. She lived with his accusations all Sunday afternoon. She let him rage without a word and quietly returned back to church on Sunday night.

One early Sunday morning when he was vomiting on the new wool rug in the living room she firmly declared "Clyde, this is the last mess I'm cleaning up!" This 6-foot oil-field-strong man *heard* his 5-foot petite wife. It was the last mess Myrtle cleaned and the last mess Clyde made.

However, the battle continued. One Sunday noon Myrtle came home walking on air. She had seen some of the people she had been praying for accept the Lord that morning at an altar of prayer. She had gone up to pray with them and they had prayed through to glorious victory.

The cool spring air touched her soft skin as she stepped out of that little church. God was so good and no joy could compare to that of a person accepting the Lord. She quickly walked the few blocks home and opened the front door with the long glass in the center. The smell of roast beef, carrots, and potatoes permeated the house. She began spreading the white damask tablecloth, putting out her china she had collected from DUZ dish soap, and gathering her little family of four for Sunday dinner.

Clyde suddenly roared into the kitchen. "Myrtle," he growled in an accusing voice with fire in his eyes, "I peeked in the window up at the church this morning. I saw you up at the altar praying, and the preacher had his hand clean up your dress." Myrtle tried to reason with him, but found the battle only became hotter. She discovered she couldn't reason or argue with jealousy, so she kept quiet.

Vera, Myrtle's daughter, began attending church with her. One night to Myrtle's delight she saw 16-year-old Vera make her way down the sawdust floor church to the altar to ask Jesus to forgive her sins.

For seven years Myrtle had been the only believer in her immediate and extended family. To have her daughter join her was the answer to many prayers. Vera grew rapidly in the faith and upon graduation from high school felt God calling her into the ministry.

She had an outstanding voice. Having won some local competitions, her voice teacher thought she could go far in this career. After much prayer Vera sensed God calling her to a little-known Bible college in Colorado Springs. So at the next voice lesson she broke the news to her teacher. Throwing up her hands in disgust and disappointment she blurted, "You will never be known out of this county."

At the same time Clyde was fuming and making threats. Being financially capable of paying the entire tuition, he refused to pay a dime. Coupled with this, he told Myrtle that Vera absolutely could not go. Furthermore, if he came home from work and found Vera gone, he would kill her. Myrtle knew his threats were not to be taken lightly, but she also knew God.

She quickly found some housecleaning jobs. Vera worked at Woolworths and they were able to put together enough money to pay for the first semester. There was now one more piece to put together and that was the need for transportation to Colorado. Myrtle knew God would provide but Vera's faith was wavering.

They rounded up Sunshine Biscuit boxes to pack Vera's belongings with the faith that transportation would be forthcoming. A few days before departure time the phone rang.

106

"Sister Carter," the voice boomed over the wire, "this is Brother Doll. Wife and I are going to Colorado Springs next week and I just felt the Lord wanted me to call you." Myrtle began to shout praises to God over the phone and related the events to him.

As Vera kissed her godly mother good-bye that late August morning, her father's threats raced through her mind, accompanied by pictures of his past behavior. Yet she looked forward to the future God had promised her. Blinded with tears, she crawled into the car, certain of her mother's prayers and her own fledgling faith in the God who provided.

Clyde walked in the door that night already angry. It was as if he had a sixth sense that told him he had lost the battle. Immediately looking for Myrtle he shouted, "Where is she?" Myrtle looked him straight in the eyes and firmly said, "She's gone to Bible school." Rage broke loose! He lunged for her throat. Something stopped him! "It was like a shield surrounded me," Myrtle said later. "His eyes were filled with hate and he would come at me with both hands and then stop." He repeated this several times. Finally, he walked away, cursing uncontrollably. His most violent act that hot August night was to go all over the house and turn every picture of Vera toward the wall.

Myrtle continued to clean houses and send a few dollars to Vera in school. The church people were also supportive emotionally and spiritually. In a few months Clyde started asking questions about Vera. Then Myrtle noticed a picture in a back room had been turned around. By Christmas all the pictures had been turned "facing out" again and Clyde began talking about how good it would be if Vera came home for Christmas. The house was decorated for Christmas and the air hung heavy with the aroma of freshly baked oatmeal cookies. Myrtle could not believe the words she heard from the living room. One of Clyde's working partners had dropped in and Clyde bragged, "This here picture is of my daughter. She attends a Bible school in Colorado Springs and we're expecting her home in a few days."

Myrtle knew only God could change the hearts of people. Little did she know how God was preparing her for another job in her life journey.

Clyde had stopped drinking. The jealousy was subsiding, but he still would not accompany her to church. "Well Myrtle," he smugly said one night, "I've been transferred. You'll be 35 miles from church and you can't drive." Myrtle's heart sank, but then she remembered how faithful God had been over the years and He would not fail her now. In fact she started singing that song by Bessie Hatcher:

> "He stills the storms and
> He calms my fears,
> He forgave my sins and
> He dries my tears,
> He is the same through endless years,
> He will not fail me now."

All the unpacking done, she knew she was going to like this little house, but Clyde was right. It was going to be impossible to attend church. Her thoughts turned toward her large extended family, still without the Lord.

In a few weeks the call came that her mother was dying of cancer and needed care. Myrtle was the one selected to care for her in her dying days. Her mother accepted the Lord and they enjoyed sweet fellowship in her last days.

Five white houses trimmed with kelly green stood in a row in this oil lease. Myrtle made friends with all of her neighbors and started a Sunday school in her living room for the children. Soon the adults joined them.

This was a bit more than Clyde had bargained for – church right in his own living room!

Clyde's mother began to fail in health. She had been living with her daughter and was such a fiesty person they refused to continue taking care of her. Clyde offered his home and assured the family Myrtle could handle anything.

Alice Carter moved in. This now ninety-plus-year-old woman was still the tough, hardhearted person who ran the covered wagon into Oklahoma to claim land. She definitely wanted nothing to do with Myrtle's religion. But Myrtle was not the least bit phased by her cursing and snorting. She tenderly and firmly took care of her needs and read the scriptures out loud to her every morning.

Slowly the crusty shell began to fall from her spirit and one morning while reading scripture, tears began to fall down her thin, wrinkled face. Her piercing black eyes looked into Myrtle's and she said, "Myrtle, He touched me on my hand." She lived on for two more years and they had great times of prayer and praise together. Alice grew in the Lord. Her patience with pain was incomprehensible and the beauty of Christ was revealed through this woman who only came to know the Lord in her nineties.

Vera beautifully sang the gospel song, "The Touch of His Hand on Mine," at Alice's funeral and Vera's minister husband preached the service.

Relatives came and went from the green-and-white house on the lease. It became a place of peace and hope for the alcoholic nephew, the promiscuous niece, the frazzled pastor's wife's daughter, the over-extended businessman's son, the tough oil driller brothers and many more whom God dropped along the way for a period of twenty-plus years.

Clyde mellowed over these years and began attending church with her occasionally. She knew God was guiding in every detail and regularly praised Him for it.

Their retirement home in Hutchinson, Kansas was located across the street from the Kansas District Pilgrim Campground. Myrtle literally thought she had moved to heaven. She could now go to church every time the doors opened. Clyde began accompanying her more and more. She had always wanted to teach a pre-school Sunday school class and it wasn't long before this opportunity came. Clyde started doing odd jobs around the church and found out that preachers weren't as bad as he had imagined.

In fact, as he talked of his ideas of preachers, it was obvious how Satan had filled his mind with deception. Slowly he was beginning to see truth.

The Hutchinson home was filled with good times of family gatherings, grandchildren, church dinners, good camp meeting services, and Clyde's mellowing.

Myrtle began to see her extended family come to the Lord one by one. The conversations around the big mahogany table consisted more and more of the walk of faith and less and less of gossip and material longings. Clyde began contributing to their conversations and his hunger became more obvious.

Retirement became a struggle for Clyde. He smoked more and enjoyed it less. However, he turned to Myrtle more and more. He found in her a tower of strength he knew he did not possess.

One fall day Myrtle heard a cry from the living room. She rushed from the kitchen and found Clyde lying unconscious on the floor. He recovered from the stroke, but more importantly, he gave his heart to God. They enjoyed the scriptures and prayer together for several months. One day she asked, "Clyde, why did you wait so long?" With regret and disappointment he said, "I always thought I needed to quit smoking before I came to the Lord."

After Clyde's death, Myrtle still had plenty to learn. She did not know how to drive nor had she ever written a check.

Her children and grandchildren all lived hundreds of miles away. So at sixty-six years of age she took a driver's training course, passed with good scores, and got a driver's license. One weekend course from her son and daughter in bookkeeping started her on her journey of personal finance. She even traded cars and actually made a "good deal." She always gave all the praise and glory for any of her accomplishments to her Lord.

Vera came to visit one summer to find Myrtle had a great-nephew living with her. He had been in trouble, serving some time in a state reformatory and needed more than secular rehabilitation. Her body now shrunken and her arthritic hands more curled, she still continued serving God's children with the same energy, enthusiasm, and hope.

"A precious thing in the Lord's sight is the death of those who die faithful to him" (Psalm 115:15-16).

As I looked at my grandmother in her casket, December 1982, I knew God had inspired that passage with her in mind. She had finally gone to join her baby – and many others – to rejoice forever around the throne of God.

Dovie Glover Gibson

by Mary Faith G. Jennings

Trust and obey, for there's no other way to be happy in Jesus, but to trust and obey." My mother, Dovie Glover Gibson, sang those words and lived by them. Born in York County, South Carolina, on October 18, 1880, she went to be with the Lord on February 28, 1978. Her life was dedicated completely to God, to love and serve Him in every way possible. Both my mother and father determined early in their marriage to put Christ first in all things. To aid them in this desire and decision, God directed them to a group of Wesleyan Methodists who were meeting in the homes in the community to which they had moved. They began worshiping with these earnest Christians, finding joy and peace in Christ for which their hearts had longed. They became members of what is now known as the First Wesleyan Church of Gastonia, North Carolina, in 1902 and served faithfully in different positions throughout their lives.

Since I am the eleventh of twelve children in our family, you can well understand that there was much activity all the time. While my father worked during the day and lived his faith, my mother was a consistent witness at home and in the neighborhood.

Since Christ was the center of their home, Dovie and her husband, Baxter, were faithful in teaching their children the Word of God and the importance of applying it to their lives. Deuteronomy 6:7 was daily practiced: "Impress them [these commandments] on your children. Talk about them when you sit at home and when you walk along the road, when you lie down and when you get up." (NIV) Dovie would sing and pray as she prepared the meals at her woodburning kitchen range or while scrubbing the clothes on the washboard, unless one of her seven daughters was available for the task.

As newer appliances were made available and finances permitted, better equipment for the home was supplied. Whatever the circumstances and whatever her task, Dovie would sing to the Lord. By her example and teaching, these privileges were taught her children and the principles of Christian living were instilled in their hearts. "The Great Physician" by William Hunter was one of her favorite songs: "The Great Physician now is near, the sympathizing Jesus; He speaks the drooping heart to cheer, . . . Your many sins are all forgiven. . . . Go on your way in peace to heaven, and wear a crown with Jesus. His Name dispels my guilt and fear, No other name but Jesus; Oh! how my soul delights to hear the charming name of Jesus."

Some of the "rules of the roost," as her oldest daughter, Carrie McKee, termed them, were:

1. No slang or "ugly" words.
2. No one saying, "Shut up!"
3. No quarreling between children.
4. No talking back to parents.
5. No leaving home without permission.
6. No disciplining of younger siblings by older ones.
7. Regular church attendance – Sunday mornings and evenings and prayer meeting on Wednesday night. If someone was unable to go to church on Sunday morning, there would be no activity during the day.
8. Faithfully pay the tithe.
9. No misbehaving in church.
10. Proper respect to be shown for older people. No first names. Use "Ma'am" or "Sir" when addressing adults.
11. No criticism of teachers. Expect another spanking at home if one was received at school.
12. Come straight home from school!
13. No dating until sixteen years of age.
14. Eat everything on your plate.
15. If food is limited, take only your share.

In addition to the "rules of the roost," giving thanks for meals and nightly family prayer times were always practiced. After each person prayed, the family repeated together "the Lord's prayer."

Tithing, also, was always strictly practiced, since God instructed in Malachi 3:10: " 'Bring the whole tithe into the

114

storehouse. . . . Test me in this,' says the Lord Almighty, 'and see if I will not throw open the flood gates of heaven and pour out so much blessing that you will not have room enough for it' " (NIV). Interestingly enough, when our cow became very ill, my parents discussed it with the minister. His immediate question was, "Do you have a cushion to kneel on?" (meaning, "Are your tithes paid?") When the question was understood, the quick answer was, "Yes!" Prayer was offered and God caused the cow to recover. What a beautiful relationship between a loving heavenly Parent and obedient children!

One of my mother's favorite scripture verses was Philippians 4:19: "But my God shall supply all your need according to His riches in glory by Christ Jesus." This was definitely a great need in a family of our size. In addition, there was an adopted thirteen-year-old cousin who needed protection and spiritual guidance. Dovie's oldest son's wife died, making it necessary for him to bring his three children back "home" with him so that he could continue to work for their care. All during her married life, there were others who needed a home for a time and this was supplied as much as possible.

Dovie did not have the privilege of much formal education, but it was amazing to see how God taught her His ways, giving daily instruction in her walk with Him and in her service for Him. Dovie was always eager to learn, making every effort to be a supportive wife and mother. She instinctively understood situations that might not have been explained completely and always had an understanding attitude. This attitude inspired trust and gave her children the desire to talk with her about any situation that arose. Her insight into human nature helped her give valuable counsel, and her teaching was so thorough that her family respected it and lived it.

Dovie was very consistent in her teaching in the discipline of her family, but, perhaps, a little too tolerant in following through with her threats. There were, however, times when she was pushed into backing up her threats. At such times, she would use a four-barreled gun, sending the child after the switch to be used, having a long talk about the necessity of the punishment, administering the punishment, and then praying together for God's help in that situation. Usually it was very effective and helped the recipient to promise to do better. Discipline was never administered in anger, another evidence of God's grace in Dovie's heart.

Since their church was the center of family activities, it was natural to have the pastor and his family, visiting missionaries, and evangelists in their home. Dovie and Baxter loved to entertain as many of the church leaders as possible because they felt that contacts of this nature would be influential in the lives of their growing family. This proved to be true as the family came to know and respect many godly people. On one occasion, Dr. Roy S. Nicholson spent a Saturday night in their home. That night it snowed eight to ten inches. The Gibson family lived almost two miles from the church. Since Dr. Nicholson was scheduled to preach that morning and driving seemed impossible, he felt he should begin walking to church. Baxter used an up-turned wheelbarrow to make tracks for the car down the hill to the road to enable him to at least begin the drive to the church!

Since Dovie felt very keenly her lack of education, she made certain that each child had the opportunity for an education, including instruction in music. Since the Child Labor Law had not yet been put into effect when the older children were growing up, they worked in the cotton mill to help with family finances. It was agreed they would take turns going to Central Wesleyan College for their high school and college education and then help another one the next year. Quite a lesson in cooperation! In addition to this, the older ones helped with the musical instruction and education of the younger ones.

One special family activity we all enjoyed greatly was gathering in the living room for a family hymn sing. The four oldest daughters furnished the music by playing the piano, violin, saxophone, and clarinet. They would also play for church services since this was the reason for their instruction.

As Dovie was growing up, her father had played the fiddle for community square dances. Because of this, she was exposed to the wicked results of swearing, drinking alcoholic beverages, and the evils associated with dancing. As a result, Dovie warned her family very sternly against these evils and strongly encouraged them to use their talents for Christ and His church.

Dovie was married at the age of seventeen and left home before her father died a year later. It was not until she was about eighty years of age that one of her sisters mentioned in conversation that their father had asked many times to have the Bible read to him before he died. Because of this, Dovie felt some hope that perhaps her father had become a Christian before he died; and if so, she would see him in heaven.

When she was married in 1898, the only wedding gift was a one-legged hen! In 1901, they moved from the farm to Gastonia, North Carolina. Life was very different from today. It was much more difficult to accomplish the basic tasks. They had no electricity, no running water, no modern appliances, no central heating, and a path out the back door to the out-house.

One day in 1902, Dovie wanted to help a sick neighbor. She took her two young sons along, since there was no one to care for them. When she returned home, a policeman knocked on her door to inquire whether anyone had been to visit the sick neighbors. He then told her that the neighbors had smallpox and that Dovie and the boys would have to be vaccinated against smallpox and be under quarantine for three weeks. Dovie was expecting her third child and could not have the vaccination! What could they do? Mr. Dalton, a lay leader in their church, told Dovie and her husband to read Psalm 91. Verses 2, 5, 9-11 stood out to them: "I will say of the Lord, 'He is my refuge and my fortress, my God, in whom I trust. You will not fear the terror of night, nor the arrow that flies by day, nor the pestilence that stalks in the darkness, nor the plague that destroys it at midday. If you make the Most High your dwelling – even the Lord who is my refuge – then no harm will befall you, no disaster will come near your tent. For He will command His angels concerning you to guard you in all your ways." After having read God's Word and prayed in faith believing, they trusted God to deliver them from this dreaded and usually fatal disease. God kept His Word and they were delivered!

Dovie loved to help the sick and often volunteered to breast feed infants of nursing mothers who were too ill to feed their babies. Matthew 11:40 says, " 'I tell you the truth, what-ever you did for one of the least of these . . . you did it for me.' " She kept one set of twins for several weeks because their mother was seriously ill. Later, she fed "Little Joe," a baby whose mother died in childbirth. Bottle feeding was not available during those years and so finding another "mother" was a serious necessity.

On one occasion, a young girl in the community fell ill. The doctor had been called but he didn't have any hope of the girl's recovery. Dovie learned of the situation, took a hot water bottle, heated some bricks to wrap and place around the girl to keep her body warm, and then stroked the girl's extremities to stimulate circulation, praying all the time for the Lord's help. When the doctor returned, expecting that the girl would have died, he found that she was showing signs of improvement. The girl recovered completely.

The "Gibson filling station" was the nickname for Dovie's home which was conveniently located near the highway used in traveling to Central Wesleyan College, Central, South Carolina. Many times students on their way to or from the college would stop by for a snack since there was very little spending money and few places to spend it. One day the telephone rang informing the family that a group of seventeen college students would be stopping by for lunch. The family had just been seated, but with that news everyone jumped up from the table to save the food for the ones coming. No one complained about those unexpected visits, for there was a very deep interest in the college and the students attending there.

Dovie and her husband felt so strongly about the importance of Christian education at our church college that all the family plus the adopted daughter were students at Central Wesleyan College, either in high school or college. They made many sacrifices to make this possible and God honored their efforts by giving them a Christian family. Two of the daughters became missionaries, serving in Colombia, South America, India, and Sierra Leone, West Africa. Other daughters served as a teacher, a pastor's wife, and a YMWB director for about twenty-five years. The other children served the Lord and the church in various other capacities.

Even though Dovie felt that she had no talents or abilities, her life was spent reaching out to others, sharing Christ's love and showing His plan of salvation with the hope that many others would join her in heaven with Christ. One of the projects she most enjoyed was preparing boxes for missions. Collecting the articles, laundering or cleaning, repairing, replacing buttons and zippers on the used clothes, packing, and sending the boxes were jobs done as carefully as possible and done as unto the Lord. These boxes were sent to mountain missions in North Carolina, Brainerd Indian School in South Dakota, and overseas mission work.

When Dovie heard about a young lady in the area of the North Carolina mountain missions who had a deep desire to go to college in order to become a teacher, but didn't have money to purchase the clothing necessary, she enlisted the help of other church ladies and sent clothes to Eunice during the entire four-year period she was in school.

While most of her family were still at home, with many mouths to feed, two women from the neighborhood went to Dovie's house one very rainy day to "borrow" a gallon of buttermilk. The older children at home tried to persuade her to refuse. But Dovie thought about the words of Luke 6:35: ". . . and do good, and lend, hoping for nothing again; and your reward will be great. . . ." She felt it was her Christian opportunity and duty to comply with their request. After all, Ecclesiastes 11:1 instructs us to "Cast your bread upon the waters, for after many days you will find it again." God had proved himself faithful on so many occasions and how gracious He had been!

In spite of limited resources and education, Dovie knew how to stretch what she had. When families moved into her neighborhood who were not accustomed to attending church or did not recognize their need for God, she immediately visited them and invited them to accompany her to church. If they responded, "We don't have a way to get there," she invited them to ride along with her. If they argued, "Our clothes are not good enough," she would begin finding good used clothes for them. She never permitted excuses to hinder her from promoting God's kingdom. When a project required extra finances, her husband would say, "I don't know how we can afford it, but we'll try."

One young girl, Marie, the oldest in her family, responded to Dovie's interest in her and became a true Christian. Dovie loved Marie as a Christian "mother" and helped her grow in her Christian life. Among other things, Dovie made Marie's dress for high school graduation since she was not able to purchase one. Marie was responsible for nominating Dovie as "Lady of the Hour" for Radio Station WBI, Charlotte, North Carolina, on May 19, 1949. In her letter to the radio station, Marie wrote: "Before her community had a church of its own, Mrs. Dovie Gibson took other children along with her own to church on Sundays. This lady's home is always open to anyone, and she still spreads good will by visiting the sick, sending clothes to the needy, and comforting bereaved families." At that time, Dovie was sixty-nine years of age. The following year, Marie nominated Dovie as "North Carolina Mother of the Year," including in her letter of nomination the statement, "She has been an angel of mercy to many in every community where she has resided." These expressions of appreciation were made to show Marie's love for a lady whose life had been instrumental in bringing her into God's family.

When Dovie was ninety years of age, her church voted to build a new building on the property where the old building was located. Of any of the members of the church who might have resented tearing down the old building, it might have been Dovie for her husband had helped build the very first church building on that corner. That was not the case. She knew the need and felt keenly that God's work must go forward. To be able to help with the finances, she asked for and received discontinued samples of upholstery and drapery fabrics to use in making cushions and covering three-gallon ice cream containers to be used as magazine holders or waste paper baskets. From the sale of these she was able to give an offering of five hundred dollars for one year to the building fund of the church.

Because of the size of the Gibson family, a large vegetable garden was needed for daily use as well as for canning as much as possible. Dovie loved tending her flower garden so that there would be flowers for church services each Sunday and for neighbors who might become ill. To help in this project, her husband added a greenhouse onto the south side of their home so that Dovie could keep her plants through the winter.

Christ was so important in her life that Dovie constantly found ways to tell others of His love for them and His desire to help them. Just about two weeks before Dovie went to be with her Lord, a young Christian couple visited her in her home. While they were there, she encouraged them to follow Christ completely. They were amazed at her mental alertness and spiritual concern.

Through the years, "Mama Gibson," as she was affectionately called by everyone, continued to pray with and for her family and others who visited her home. When the adult children and their families visited and departure time came, all were called together for praying, including the recitation of "the Lord's Prayer." When Dovie and Baxter celebrated their seventieth wedding anniversary, each of them gave beautiful testimonies of God's redeeming grace, goodness, and mercy throughout their married life. In Dovie's testimony, she again encouraged the family to read God's Word faithfully and have prayer each day with the children in each household.

For decades, two of Dovie's prayers were that God would permit her to live until she had raised her family and that He would let her "keep her right mind." Both of these prayers were answered. At age ninety-seven her physical health continued to fail; but mentally, she was very sharp. On Saturday night before her home-going on Tuesday morning, some of the family were having prayer with her, and she led in praying "the Lord's Prayer."

Fittingly enough, after Dr. C. Wesley Lovin had given a

most appropriate message at her funeral, encouraging each family member and friend to be sure of personal salvation, he asked the congregation to stand and pray together "the Lord's Prayer."

Throughout her life, my mother showed clearly that God's strength and grace are sufficient to meet all the challenges of life. With her very practical and consistent Christian example before me each day as I was growing up and supporting me in prayer during my college years as well as after Lowell and I were married, you can understand my love and respect for my mother.

I thank my mother for the principles that she taught me by the life that she lived.

1. Complete consecration to Christ.
2. Daily faithfulness in loving and serving Him.
3. Complete honesty; no hypocrisy.
4. Tolerance and respect for others.
5. God-given interest in others.
6. No destructive criticism.
7. Desire to be an understanding and cooperative wife and mother, creating stability and security within the home.
8. Willingness to do what might be requested if at all possible.
9. Sharing without jealousy or complaint.
10. Using God-given ingenuity as situations develop, accepting each emergency with control and finding a workable solution if at all possible.

My prayer is that God will lead me daily in His paths, working through me as He did through my mother, Dovie Glover Gibson.

Ruby Reisdorph

by Kathryn Hillen

"Come right in! I've been looking forward to meeting you!" Her wonderful smile, extended hands, and emphasis on the *you,* affirmed her greeting. It was mid-November of 1941 at the home of Rev. and Mrs. Rufus Reisdorph in Aberdeen, South Dakota. Newlyweds, John and I were visiting his brother Henry and wife, Mae (Reisdorph) Hillen, a sister of Rufus. I was uncomfortable about dropping in unannounced on a busy Saturday morning, but we were greeted with a warmth that put me at ease. Mrs. Reisdorph's gracious hospitality, known to so many, was an example to me. I took note of it, tucking it away in my mental bride's chest for future reference.

This charming woman who was to influence my life in so many ways, was born in a log cabin near Pell City, Alabama, on March 20, 1903. The third child of Mr. and Mrs. Charles Levans, Ruby weighed twelve pounds and bounced into the world equipped with two teeth. Because of her birth order in a large family, she was neither pampered nor idle. From an early age she helped with the many duties of a busy household. By the time she reached fifteen, the family had increased by two sets of twins and two singles. Ten children grew to adulthood.

Ruby remembers early spiritual yearnings. While on the playground of the village school, she would watch the fleecy clouds and wish she knew the God who made them and her. Perhaps her mother's many duties made spending time alone with individual children a virtual impossibility. At any rate,

123

Ruby found a way of communicating by writing notes to her busy mother, spelling out her spiritual questions. In a few days, carefully worded answers were returned to her. These notes, regrettably no longer available, created the special relationship shared by this wise mother and her questing child. Ruby aspired to be like her saintly mother who was obviously an excellent teacher and role model.

Music was always important in Ruby's life. She was born with natural talent and a beautiful singing voice. Eager to learn to play the family pump organ, she watched the hands of the church organist as she played the hymns, fixed the movements and positions in her mind and went home to pick out those hymn tunes. She and her sister Pearl sang well together and were singled out at an early age to sing duets in church services. Their mother wisely counseled, "If you have a voice to sing, God has given it to you. You will be held responsible to use it to glorify Him." This advice had a lasting effect on Ruby's choices. Instead of choosing worldly pursuits of fame and fortune, she used her magnificent voice to grace humble tent meetings, native huts and places of worship, camps, conferences and more small churches than large. Wherever the location, God's spirit used her musical ministry as a pivot point for many decisions for Christ and blessings for the saints.

Ruby attended church with her family and felt drawn to Christ. However, her conversion occurred in January, 1918, under the ministry of J. M. Hames. She began at once to hunger for the blessing of holiness of heart, but it was quite some time later that the light finally dawned on her soul as she was reading Hebrews 4:12.

> "For the word of God is quick and powerful and sharper than any two-edged sword, piercing even to the dividing asunder of soul and spirit, and of the joints and marrow, and is a discerner of the thoughts and intents of the heart."

As God revealed unbelief in her heart, she prayed for His cleansing and filling and was marvelously sanctified. The Bible then became a new Book to her as the Holy Spirit illumined its pages and gave interpretation.

Following graduation from high school, Ruby joined Miss Hattie Avery in mission work in Bessemer, Alabama. She was deeply committed to this endeavor which resulted in the establishing of a Wesleyan Methodist church in that area. A tent meeting was launched and Rev. and Mrs. Nathan Beskin were called as workers. Ruby labored faithfully, unaware of the changes that would result in her life as a consequence of her association with the Beskins. Impressed by the potential of three young women in the congregation, one of which was Ruby, the evangelist urged the three to attend Marion College. While the girls were contemplating this big step in their lives, the Beskins began to raise funds from the congregation for the trio's college expenses.

Though the prospect of a higher education interested her, Ruby felt a responsibility to her family and to the Bessemer work. To further complicate matters, while she was seeking God's will, a well-meaning older Christian advised her that she would be stepping out of divine order if she left the mission. The Beskins obviously had the mind of the Lord in the matter, and continued to urge the young women to enter Marion College. They even made arrangements for the girls to live in a private home near the college. God gave His approval, overcame Ruby's reluctance, and a decision was made that was to have a lifelong impact on her and many others.

The Beskins' interest was unabated. During her first year at Marion they called Ruby to be the song leader in a series of meetings they were conducting in Erie, Pennsylvania. After making arrangements to keep up with her studies while absent, she set out on a facet of her ministry that has blessed many down through the years.

Ruby often joined other students in presenting services at the city jail, and it was in that activity that she and a fellow student, Rufus Reisdorph, became friends. In modern terms, he was "big man on campus" – president of the student body and a gifted speaker and debater. In time their relationship progressed to a more-than-just-friends stage and a marriage proposal.

Not daring to be influenced solely by her deep feelings for this young man from rural South Dakota, Ruby followed her established practice of seeking God's will in the matter. She also asked the advice of her trusted Sunday school teacher. Though stating her approval of the match, the teacher advised taking a full day to seek God's direction. During that day of prayer, Ruby came to the point of resigning herself completely to God's will in this important decision. She remembers telling the Lord that His "No" would be as sweet as His "Yes" in the relationship. At this point, the Lord made it clear that He approved of the marriage.

The wedding took place in Birmingham, Alabama, on October 25, 1927, and the Reisdorphs began a long and varied

125

ministry together and, at times, separately. Notably, her husband's ministry was always given precedence by this godly woman. As his responsibilities and titles changed – evangelist, pastor, district president, general Sunday school editor and secretary, World War II chaplain, college president, general superintendent and, finally, active missionary – Ruby graciously adapted her wifely hat to accommodate each position. In every case, the Lord provided a ministry especially fitted to her time and talents. I was impressed that He still operates in that same fashion, and that, when two are made one in the Lord, their future ministries are, not necessarily identical, but always compatible.

Three years into Rev. Reisdorph's service as president of the sprawling Dakota district, he received a scholarship from Vanderbilt University in Nashville, Tennessee. The district granted a year's leave of absence, and the work was left in the capable hands of the vice president, Rev. J. T. McGovern.

The year in Nashville was rewarding. Ruby was able to resume voice training with Miss Ada B. Carroll, her former instructor at Marion College who was now on staff at Trevecca College in Nashville. The greatest blessing of that memorable year was the arrival of daughter Martha. The little family returned to Aberdeen for the completion of Rev. Reisdorph's tenure as district president, and Martha gave new flavor and joy to them and to their constituents. The Lord helped this gifted couple to take good care of their child while following a busy schedule.

In 1943, having served for twelve years as general secretary, Mrs. Reisdorph was elected general president of the Women's Missionary Society. During sixteen years in that office, several useful and innovative programs and emphases were born. Some of them are still a part of the Wesleyan Women International agenda: the prayer schedule setting aside Tuesdays as the day to unite on behalf of the needs of missions at home and abroad; prayer partners chosen from missionaries on the fields; and the Women's Prayer Fellowship, nurtured by its first secretary, Mrs. Margaret McCarty.

Though some doubted that the women would read all those books, the reading course was instituted. The ensuing years show that this promotion of carefully chosen reading materials has enlarged missionary vision for thousands, and continues to be a well-supported part of Wesleyan Women International.

In the early 1940s Rev. Reisdorph volunteered as an Army

chaplain. He was commissioned and sent to minister to the U.S. troops in the European theater of operations. When he returned, the family moved to Denver, Colorado, where he enrolled in a doctoral program.

Mrs. Reisdorph furnished their tiny home with thrift shop and garage sale items, and they lived quite frugally and happily during their Denver year. Because of her willingness to share ideas, she was a source of encouragement and practical help for me and others faced with postwar shortages. She had a way of making these challenges seem like fun.

During that same year, Mrs. Reisdorph was invited to accompany missionary Anna McGhie on a tour of the Caribbean and South American mission fields. With her husband's urging and help, and in spite of misgivings about leaving her family, she embarked on an exciting, taxing, and educational jaunt that became a concentrated course in missions. Firsthand she witnessed the extreme physical and spiritual poverty of our neighbors to the south. Going to minister as well as to observe, she thrilled to see God transforming people of darkness into vibrant Christians. As was her custom, she returned to channel this vision to the people of the Wesleyan Methodist churches in the States. None of her experiences were ever wasted, but became seeds of missions awareness planted in the hearts of the many to whom she ministered. She had a marked influence on my decision to devote much of my time to the work of the missions organizations of the church. This involvement has enriched my life and the lives of my husband and children.

While living in Houghton, New York, in 1951, the Reisdorphs were part of a great revival that began at Houghton College and spread rapidly to other places. This experience was a fitting prelude to the church's commissioning of them for a 35,000-mile world missions tour. The spirit of revival accompanied them as they visited mission fields in Africa, India, Nepal, Japan, Taiwan, Australia and points in between. Their experiences on that trip would fill a large book. Again, they returned to share the blessing, the vision and needs of people in many far away places. Some of their true stories impressed me in special ways. The story of Yangen, a Nepalese girl, was particularly meaningful.

Yangen was the daughter of a simple *sherpa,* or shepherd, who received attention as one of three who were said to have found the skin of the fabled "abominable snowman," Yeti, believed by the Nepalese to inhabit the snow-covered Himalayan peaks. Scientists from several world cities asked Nepalese officials to loan the skin for study, and invited the *sherpa* to accompany the specimen to the United States. Sir Edmund Hillary, British explorer who had put Nepal on the map with his climb of Mt. Everest, offered to accompany the group, and the government consented. The trip was eye-opening to this humble, uneducated shepherd. Impressed with the possibilities civilization had to offer, he returned to Nepal with an idea – maybe *his* daughter could learn something outside of the traditional duties of her tribe.

Drs. Robert and Bethel Fleming, administrators of the Kathmandu hospital, had impacted the shepherd's life sometime earlier. He obviously trusted them, for he chose Dr. Bethel to help him accomplish his seemingly impossible dream. One day he brought Yangen to the gate of the Kathmandu hospital compound. When Dr. Bethel greeted them, he said, "This is my daughter. I'm giving her to you. Take her and teach her something!" Dr. Bethel saw a dirty, extremely frightened child with no obvious abilities, but she accepted the challenging gift.

Yangen learned quickly, soon came to a saving knowledge of Christ, and became very useful around the hospital. She was trained to be a nurse. By the time the Reisdorphs visited there, she had greatly changed from the ignorant child Dr. Bethel had chosen to an intelligent, productive woman. Wesleyan missionary nurse, Isla Knight, introduced her to them by saying, "This is Yangen. She is to be our first Christian nurse." Listening to Yangen's story, I saw myself as I must have appeared to God, brought by our great Shepherd and presented for cleansing from sin. God's transforming power is equally amazing and observable in a life, whatever the cultural background may be. Mrs. Reisdorph had the ability to bring increased missionary vision and personal spiritual introspection to her hearers.

While in Taiwan, the Reisdorphs were invited to visit a work among the lepers. Their recounting of the sight of deformed lepers crawling or inching their way up the mountainside to their little church moved me greatly. These often shunned Christians had found acceptance from the Lord, and they were willing to sit for hours listening to stories of Jesus and His love. The lepers' joy in the Lord and their adjustment to a dreaded disease was epitomized by one Mrs. Reisdorph called 'the leper with the shining face.' Because there was something so striking about his scarred yet beaming countenance, she asked the missionary about him. She learned that he had a right to his shining face. In the past year he had won fifty-two lepers to Christ! (I felt rebuked as I compared my record to his.)

As the visitors approached their car to leave the area, a group of lepers stood at a distance and sang in broken English, "God Will Take Care of You". Mrs. Reisdorph was deeply touched by this testimony, feeling that she should be singing that song to these shining saints. Their simple faith and joy, the willingness to minister to the limit of their capacity, demonstrated that physical disability does not cancel out the opportunity for service. Indeed, availability, not ability, is the key.

In Tokyo, Japan, they met Dr. David Tsutada, leader of the Emmanuel Church and Bible school. I remember Dr. Tsutada's story well as she retold it later. Not long after World War II, ill-feeling against the Japanese people lingered in the hearts of many Americans who had lost loved ones in the South Pacific war zone. For any Christians who might have been struggling with this aftermath of the war, hearing the account of this faithful Japanese Christian had a healing effect that helped to combat the tendency to judge the entire population of that country by the actions of their leaders.

Dr. Tsutada was imprisoned simply because he preached that Christ would be coming again to reign as King of Kings and Lord of Lords. After about two years of deprivation and mistreatment, so undernourished and weak that he fully expected to die, Dr. Tsutada lay on the floor of his cell one night and prayed for a special manifestation of the Lord. Suddenly, his cell was filled with light. He knew it was the presence of the Lord. The vision concluded with the audible words, "I AM Emmanuel; I AM with you. I WILL BE with you. I WILL NEVER leave you!" At that time, he was given the vision for the church he was to build on release from captivity, a vision that helped to sustain him from that time forward.

This special lady didn't put herself on a pedestal as a person who never had fears or worries. She shared, with candor, her feelings at the time of their return flight from Tokyo to Honolulu. They were informed that they were on a plane making a test flight in the jet stream. Though she would later learn that the jet stream referred to a circumpolar wind circulating, usually, from west to east, at that time she neither understood nor felt comfortable about being part of an experiment. Sharing her humanness, while pointing out God's sufficiency in all of our fears and uncertainties, was helpful to women who all had their own little private anxieties.

129

On landing in Los Angeles and sighting the U.S. flag, Mrs. Reisdorph felt the surge of a new text gripping her heart: "I am debtor". Turning to her husband she said, "That flag is preaching to me. I feel I owe a debt to every woman in the world." That was not a momentary resolve, for she has continued to witness and minister for her Lord into her golden years as an example of obedience to the heavenly vision. To this day, whenever I am tempted to feel that I have paid my dues and deserve some time just for myself, I am reminded that, because I have been so blessed, I, too, owe a debt to the women in my world. My role may change from time to time, but I can never retire until I hear His "Well done".

In their travels in the States, the Reisdorphs were guests in the homes of many pastors and their families, and with interesting results. For example, one young pastor's wife, mother of two lively preschool-aged sons, told this story. "On arrival, Mrs. Reisdorph said, 'Now tomorrow I want you to go shopping, calling with your husband, or whatever you may choose. I will take care of the boys and the house so that you can enjoy some time off.' This service continued for the duration of their stay of almost a week. What a blessing! I really needed a break in my routine, and I'll always be grateful."

Other pastor's wives told of jelly making, baking and multiple extras done for their families during visits by one of God's choice servants who had the exemplary gift of discerning how and when she could minister most effectively.

I'll never forget the day in our home when one of Mrs. Reisdorph's lovely favors began to take shape. She was admiring our new but empty maple corner cupboard and I heard her say, "Husband, wouldn't a set of 'our' china look nice in there?" He agreed. Then she told me how much she enjoyed shopping at the Syracuse China seconds shop (no longer in business) and assembling sets of china for their friends at a small cost. Because the flaws are so tiny, this china is every bit as lovely and serviceable as first quality. I was delighted to join the long list of families who have enjoyed this courtesy. A short time later we became the owners of a beautiful service for twelve of pure white Syracuse china. These dishes have been such a help as we have enjoyed showing hospitality to many guests over the years, and they are a constant reminder of the love of a dear friend who has a servant's heart.

At the rise of the 1963 General Conference of the Wesleyan Methodist Church, Dr. Reisdorph terminated his services as a General Superintendent, but not with retirement to a rocking chair in mind. God was calling them to active missionary service in a needy field.

During their world missions tour they had visited a number of small churches in the Philippine Islands which had been built by Rev. Romeo Baronia. Baronia had worked in the sugar beet harvest in the States, and after his conversion attended God's Bible School in Cincinnati, Ohio, before returning to his homeland to evangelize his own people. Romeo's parting plea to the Reisdorphs was not unlike the Macedonian cry of St. Paul's experience, "Please come back and help us to establish a Bible school." Motivated by the Lord to answer that call, the Reisdorphs went by faith, built their own house on the mission compound, and helped to build churches and parsonages in the area. They also gave valuable leadership in establishing the Villasis Bible School where they taught classes and improved academics, buildings and housing for the national students. Mrs. Reisdorph taught a class on "Building the Home Christian" which was of great help to young couples, many of whom were going out as pastors and wives.

The work was difficult but rewarding, for the people were responsive, appreciative, and learned quickly. In a few years, the people were willing and able to assume responsibility for their own Bible school and workers' training center. Looking back on their twelve years of active missionary labors, Dr. Reisdorph observed that those were the most wonderful and fruitful years of their varied career. Choosing to refire rather than retire, this godly couple have been role models of the finest sort for others who have enjoyed an extended ministry in a new field.

About a year after returning from the Philippines, Dr. Reisdorph went to be with the Lord. His dignity in death matched that which personified him throughout his life. Following a quiet evening at home, he went out to the kitchen for a drink of water. Suddenly, as his life slipped away, he seemed more to lie down on the floor than to fall. As his faithful companion knelt at his side, she was aware of the wonderful, shining Presence of God permeating the house. In awe, she said, "Husband, the Presence of Jesus is closer than our very breath! What a wonderful way to go home, after a lifetime of service!" Naturally, there were tears later but, in the midst of her grief, God spoke. "My child, you're weeping over your loss. Why not rather count the blessings of almost half a century in the service of God – together?" She was marvelously serene as she recalled, "I began to count my blessings, and

131

I'm still counting!" And she's still serving. In a recent letter she wrote, "As the candle burns low, I realize that what I do must be done quickly. But, oh, I'm having so much joy – all the way home!"

Irene Powers
Bonnie Ogburn
George A. Cox
Andrea Cox
Helen Warren
Lucille Cox
Evelyn Younger
Barbara Hinkle
Gloria Gafford
Blanche Whitted
Marvin Whitehead
Edith Whitehead
Juanita Bradford
Emily Messer
Esther Miller
J. Cook
Betty O'Dell
Carolyn Phillips
Jennie Herron
Esther Durham
Robert Durham
Becki Frazier
John H. Barnard
Ethel C. Barnard